THE PROMISE OF BLOCKCHAIN

HOPE AND HYPE
FOR AN EMERGING
DISRUPTIVE TECHNOLOGY

JASON SCHENKER

THE PROMISE OF BLOCKCHAIN

HOPE AND HYPE FOR AN EMERGING DISRUPTIVE TECHNOLOGY

BY JASON SCHENKER

ISBN: 978-1-946197-10-8 *Paperback*
      978-1-946197-11-5 *Ebook*

For those strategists, economists, and futurists who wish to be tech savvy without catching tech fever.

CONTENTS

CONTENTS

THE PROMISE OF BLOCKCHAIN

My first in-depth exposure to blockchain occurred in May 2016, when one casual poolside conversation at a Fed off-site turned into a relentless quest for knowledge about all things related to financial technology — or FinTech — including blockchain, Bitcoin, ICOs, and other cryptocurrency topics.

By the end of 2016, I had completed a certificate in FinTech at MIT, founded a blockchain-supported startup, and created an entirely new learning institute — The Futurist Institute — to help economists, analysts, and strategists become more focused on the impact of future technology. In 2017, I performed research and wrote articles about Bitcoin, blockchain, and other cryptocurrencies. I also created courses for The Futurist Institute on the Future of Data and the Future of Finance with significant components dedicated to blockchain.

As a result of my work, I spoke on a FinTech panel at SXSW in 2017 about blockchain and Bitcoin. And I have had the privilege to speak about digital currencies on issues related to national security and defense to NATO and the US Department of Defense.

If you are interested in learning about blockchain, Bitcoin, and digital currencies, this book is a great place to start. After all, *The Promise of Blockchain: Hope and Hype for an Emerging Disruptive Technology* includes everything I learned between May 2016 and August 2018 about blockchain. It even includes the secrets I have shared with executives, with NATO, and with investors.

This book contains what I believe to be the most critical information about blockchain, Bitcoin, and cryptocurrencies. And it includes insights that I wish I had known earlier. But this is not a book about creating a blockchain or the underlying cryptography.

This is a book about context.

The main goal of *The Promise of Blockchain* is to clarify blockchain technology, corporate blockchain use cases, Bitcoin, and cryptocurrencies for people who are not experts in the field. And this book has been carefully crafted to provide digestible explanations of complex concepts. To meet these goals, I have structured a mix of data, anecdotes, and graphics to foster notions of context and relevance for what can otherwise seem to be esoteric technology or finance topics.

Acknowledgements

I want to acknowledge and thank all of the people who were involved in one way or another with the process of making this book come together. And there are some specific individuals I need to thank.

First, I want to thank **Kerry Ellis**, who did an amazing job producing the cover for *The Promise of Blockchain*. Her patience and support in putting together a fantastic cover with the burning Library of Alexandria framed by a digital binary chain was greatly appreciated.

I also wish to thank **Nawfal Patel** and my other colleagues at Prestige Economics, as well as everyone at Prestige Professional Publishing, who helped me bring this book to fruition.

Finally, and most importantly, I want to thank my family for supporting me as I worked on this book. I dedicated previous books to my loving wife, **Ashley Schenker,** and to my unflappable parents, **Jeffrey and Janet Schenker**. Although I have dedicated this book *"For those strategists, economists, and futurists who wish to be tech savvy without catching tech fever,"* it is my family that has supported me in countless ways over the years by providing emotional support and editorial feedback. Every time I write a book, it's a crazy experience that spills over into my family life, so to them and to everyone else who helped me in this process: thank you!

And of course, thank you for buying this book. I hope you enjoy *The Promise of Blockchain*!

HOPE AND HYPE FOR AN EMERGING DISRUPTIVE TECHNOLOGY

Complicated economic and financial issues require nuance, but there has been little room for nuance in the world of blockchain.

Don't believe me? Try adding the word blockchain anywhere on your LinkedIn profile and watch what kind of traction and messages your profile gets.

Yet nuance and discourse are how real understanding happens. This has directly influenced the structure of this book as well as the title. The title, *The Promise of Blockchain*, indicates big hopes as well as big expectations for blockchain technology. In short, blockchain is a new kind of database that can allow for more transparency, clearer custody of ownership, and distributed use of that data. I will discuss these important nuts and bolts of blockchain in Chapter 3: Anatomy of a Blockchain.

There are many value propositions for blockchain technology, but the biggest value for blockchain, in my opinion, is its reduction of risks that present a central point of failure.

I discuss the importance of a central point of failure as a centralized kind of single point of failure in Chapter 3. In short, a single point of failure exists in a system, where if one point breaks, the entire system fails. Consider a major regional power grid that could fail if one specific transformer fails. Boom! With that one single point of failure, everything fails.

A central point of failure is a single point of failure that threatens the existence of an entire system because of centralization. A centralized exposure and concentration in the system threatens the entire system. A great example of a central point of failure was the burning of the ancient Library of Alexandria by Caesar during the Alexandrian Wars. Up to half a million scrolls of papyrus perished, with massive amounts of knowledge from the ancient world, when the world's leading depository of records and writings burned.

When you picked up this book, you might have wondered: What is that on the cover?

Blockchain promises to be the antithesis of a central point of failure, which is why the cover of *The Promise of Blockchain* shows the burning of the ancient Library of Alexandria.

The origins of the blockchain and its first applied use — Bitcoin — are mysterious, and I cover this topic in Chapter 4. We discuss this origin as well as the economics and theoretical rationale behind cryptocurrencies in Chapters 5 and 6, respectively.

But Bitcoin is not the only cryptocurrency, and it is not the only digital or cryptocurrency built on a blockchain. In Chapter 7, I explore the basics about other cryptocurrencies and initial coin offerings. Since not everyone understands the difference between blockchain, Bitcoin, ICOs, and other cryptocurrencies, this is a critical chapter for getting the basics down.

Hope and Hype

There has been a recent groundswell of expectations for what blockchain technology will mean for the economy, for businesses, and for investors. This is a core topic of exploration of this book — to examine the *promise* of blockchain: what it may offer and what people think it will offer.

Of course, there's also a reason why this book is subtitled *Hope and Hype for an Emerging Disruptive Technology*. The truth is that although blockchain technology has been around for a number of years, the focus on it has just begun to reach a critical mass. Much of this has been driven by the outsized financial returns early investors have seen from Bitcoin, ICOs, and other digital currencies in the past year. But both the hope — and the hype — for blockchain goes well beyond cryptocurrencies.

To bring the topic of Bitcoin and cryptocurrencies a bit more to life, I share some anecdotes and discuss some of the context for risk for Bitcoin and cryptocurrencies in Chapters 8, 9, and 10.

In Chapters 11 and 12, respectively, I focus on two important points of hype and risk represented by cryptocurrency blockchains and Bitcoin: "trustless trust" and "bloat."

One of the biggest risks for Bitcoin is that mobsters, terrorists, anarchists, and political bad actors are likely using various cryptocurrencies to their benefit. The interplay between crypto and fake news that I lay out in Chapter 12 comes from talks I have given to NATO and the Department of Defense.

Emerging Technology

Despite its existence for almost a decade, blockchain is still an emerging, disruptive technology — and there is a lot of misunderstanding and confusion that surrounds the subject. In short, blockchain is like a combustion engine. In the way that a combustion engine can be used in any number of different vehicles, blockchain technology can be as well.

In short, a blockchain is a kind of database with specialized permissions and data sharing that has significant value for corporations and society. These go well beyond blockchain's use as the engine behind so-called cryptocurrencies. This issue is the subject of Chapter 13, which also ties back into the notion of blockchain's potential to reduce central point of failure risks.

See under: The Library of Alexandria.

Burning.

Blockchain is the technology behind the biggest financial bubble in history: Bitcoin. But it is a lot more than that.

Nevertheless, there will be some industries that may face challenges using blockchain technology. Real estate and healthcare are just two areas where significant challenges will need to be addressed. This is a stark contrast to logistics, manufacturing, and freight, where blockchain is an almost ideal fit. These industries are discussed in Chapter 14.

In Chapter 15, I address the at-times crazy investing climate that has generated so much hype around blockchain to the point where the US Securities and Exchange Commission (SEC) has had to weigh in on even using the word blockchain in the name of a company.

Disruptive But Not Different

This time is never different. And that is also true of blockchain. While blockchain is likely to disrupt some traditional business models and finance operations, it is not a completely unique technology, nor is it likely to be permanent. In Chapter 17, I offer a historical context for blockchain and its place in a long-term trend of database innovation and development.

In the final chapter — Chapter 18 — I address the potential risks that quantum computing poses for cryptocurrencies and blockchains, especially in light of quantum computing's potential for codebreaking. This threat is also shown on the cover. Traditional computing on what quantum physicists and engineers call Turing machines (or normal computers) is based on binary code, with 1s and 0s. This is essentially an on and off toggle. The binary chain links that frame the cover of this book reflect the current basis of blockchain and Bitcoin cryptography.

But this also hints at future challenges. This is because quantum computing doesn't use binary code, because quantum computers have a third state of being, where there is on, off, and both on and off at the same time. This is a deep topic that we will explore in Chapter 18. It is likely to be critical for cryptography, blockchain, Bitcoin, and other digital currencies in the future.

Questions Need Answers

I have outlined a number of topics in this book. But at the end of the day, the point of the book is to provide valuable information to the reader and to answer some of the most critical questions facing anyone wishing to explore or become an expert in blockchain, Bitcoin, or cryptocurrencies.

To fulfill this goal, much of the book will be focused on answering some of the most important questions that we should be looking at, including the following:

- **What is blockchain?**

- **How is blockchain different from Bitcoin and other cryptocurrencies?**

- **What are the risks from cryptocurrencies?**

- **What are the potential corporate and societal value propositions represented by blockchain?**

- **What's next for blockchain and crypto?**

After reading *The Promise of Blockchain: Hope and Hype for an Emerging Disruptive Technology*, you will understand why I chose each word of the title and subtitle of this book. And you should be able to answer all of these questions. I explicitly define some of these terms and differences in Chapter 1, but throughout the book I have included some graphics, original research, analogies, and anecdotes that will make these topics easy to understand — and easy to explain to others.

To make sure that you get all of the topics I cover in this book, I have also included a glossary as an appendix to this book. This should serve as a handy reference to understand the headline concepts of blockchain, Bitcoin, and cryptocurrencies.

Now, let's talk about why I wrote this book.

18   THE PROMISE OF BLOCKCHAIN

CHAPTER 1

WHY I WROTE THIS BOOK

People are confused.

They are confused about what blockchain is, how it is different from Bitcoin, and what ICOs and cryptocurrencies are. Plus, many executives are still struggling to grasp what blockchain technology may mean for their businesses.

Many blockchain books have been written, but they clearly aren't doing the trick. In fact, I have read countless blockchain books, white papers, and articles over the past two years as part of my work — and in preparation for this book. But none of them was really comprehensive.

Some books focus purely on creating the technology of blockchain. Others are all about Bitcoin and getting rich quick. And yet others are now dated because blockchain technology is almost a decade old — even though its application and use cases are still emerging.

Before we get started, let's clarify a few things in basic terms.

Q: What is Blockchain?

A: Blockchain is a kind of database technology that allows for records to be distributed. This chain of records and the amount of details — like who has access and how secure it is — can be customized. Blockchain is a bit like an inverse cloud with a push element, a distributed ledger, and complex cryptography. It was first used to support Bitcoin, but it can be used for many things.

Q: What is Bitcoin?

A: It is one of the first digital currencies, and it emerged in 2009. Bitcoin fever caused massive price spikes in late 2017 that were followed by a collapse of what has been assessed to be the biggest financial asset bubble in history. Bitcoin is not backed by any bank. It is not tied to gold. It is "its own thing" and floats against fiat currencies like the dollar, yen, euro, and pound.

Q: What are ICOs?

A: Initial Coin Offerings (ICOs) are an extension of crowdfunding. They represent a way to raise capital, but these are highly speculative assets that are often tied to a pre-revenue, startup, or non-existent entity. They can involve the issue of coins or tokens.

Q: What is Crypto?

A: Cryptocurrencies, formally known as digital currencies and informally called "crypto," are any of the non-fiat, non-government currencies that trade. This includes Bitcoin and other more established coins like Ethereum and Ripple, as well as coins that have been created in lesser known ICOs.

These four questions are the main reasons I wrote this book.

I get asked about this stuff all the time, and I needed something I could just hand people to answer their questions. If I handed you this book, and you've made it this far, congratulations!

The good news is that if all you take away from this book are the answers to these four questions, my job is done here. It's that fundamental, because people should know what blockchain, Bitcoin, and cryptocurrencies are — although many do not.

To wit: Every year I go to the invite-only Atlanta Fed's Financial Markets Conference. It's one of the most impressive groups of attendees at any conference or professional boondoggle I go to. Multiple Fed Bank Presidents attend, central bankers from other countries are there, heads of financial exchanges, policymakers, CEOs of hedge funds and banks — and I've even seen Fed Chairmen there.

In May 2016, I was skipping out on a session of this conference to go to the pool, where a reporter casually explained their beat to me: FinTech. "It's like Bitcoin and stuff," the reporter explained.

I soon learned that FinTech fundamentally threatened my business, Prestige Economics, so I became an expert on it as quickly as possible. Some of the key cornerstones of FinTech are blockchain technology and cryptocurrencies — like Bitcoin. Of course, there are many other cryptocurrencies now as well, including Ethereum, Litecoin, and Ripple, just to name a few.

Between 2016 and 2018, I became an expert in FinTech, blockchain, Bitcoin, and cryptocurrencies. I completed a FinTech certificate at MIT, and I recorded multiple courses for The Futurist Institute referencing blockchain technology and its importance for data — and valuable corporate application beyond cryptocurrencies.

Of course, I also wrote articles on these subjects, I spoke at SXSW about them, and I even gave speeches to NATO and the Department of Defense on the topics of Bitcoin, cryptocurrency, and fake news.

By the time of the Atlanta Fed Financial Markets Conference in May 2018, it was painfully clear how far behind some of the CEOs, central bankers, economists, and financial thought leaders were. They were clearly not that deep into FinTech.

But they needed to be.

One speaker talked about the hacking risks on cryptocurrency exchanges and the vulnerabilities of wallets, where people keep their cryptocurrency balances. It was a fairly direct presentation, but afterward I heard multiple people ask about the difference between blockchain and Bitcoin. I even heard one person ask if Ethereum was a kind of Bitcoin.

These are all valid questions, but given the level of sophistication of the attendees at this event (and the fact that it was 2018), I was still surprised.

Maybe I should have written this book in 2017, but at the time I prioritized writing articles, giving speeches, and recording courses on these subjects for The Futurist Institute rather than writing an entire book.

But after that conference in May 2018, this book was clearly needed.

This is why I wrote this book: to help people understand important concepts and terms for which familiarity is no longer optional.

CHAPTER 2

ANATOMY OF A BLOCKCHAIN

Where does a blockchain come from?

In essence, a blockchain is a chain of individual transactions or records that are processed in blocks. These blocks become part of a permanent ledger of record that is shared in a distributed network. In this chapter I will discuss all of these concepts.

Basically, a blockchain is a kind of database.

Everything new is old. And this is also true of blockchain. Databases and recordkeeping have been around for millennia. In fact, some of the first recorded writings are based on transactional records. So it should be no surprise that advances in technology that advance transactional recordkeeping would be important — or that they would be continually improving.

Even blockchain is not a "new" concept anymore. After all, the first official Bitcoin transaction that was implemented using blockchain technology occurred in January 2009.

We need to explore the parts of a blockchain, and the best way to do this is visually. Take a look at the illustration in Figure 2-1.

Each transaction is a **record**, whether we are talking about the transfer of a Bitcoin, a physical transport load, or a piece of property. There is a buyer and a seller, and this transaction is part of an individual record.

The record then becomes part of a **block** of transactions. That's the block in the word *block*chain. These records of transactions in the block are processed together as a block. Then they are added to a chain of previously processed blocks.

The **chain** in the word block*chain*, refers to the entire history of the blocks of processed records. This history — the entire blockchain — is then distributed as a ledger to its network.

Figure 2-1: Anatomy of a Blockchain

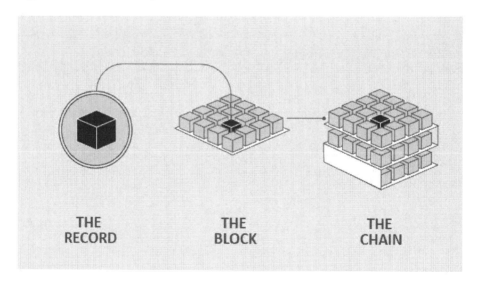

THE RECORD   THE BLOCK   THE CHAIN

An ideal blockchain, like the first one used with Bitcoin, puts transactions permanently on the blockchain, so that they cannot be altered.

Best in a Distributed Network

There are a few caveats about a blockchain that help elucidate its usefulness and purpose. This first of these is that blockchain works best in a distributed network.

In Figure 2-2, you can see what a distributed network looks like. It's when you have a number of different parties engaging in transactions, and there is no central organization to the nature of these transactions. This is like what happens with regionalized businesses or what might happen with how members of a family might spend their income. You have independence of actions and no natural central repository for all records.

Figure 2-2: Distributed Network

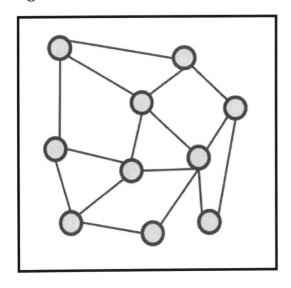

Of course, a set of records can be created and shared with a distributed network for any kind of transaction. But this has historically proved clunky.

Anyone who's ever been CC'd on an email chain for a major project knows how difficult it can be to keep track of every update. Plus, sometimes the wrong files are updated, and this can lead to errors. When I worked in management consulting at McKinsey between 2007 and 2009, this was referred to as version control. And it was a major risk in almost any project or client engagement.

Sometimes people would update the wrong file, and then important documents were at risk of being incomplete, or they would require complicated reconciliation and review.

This is also a problem with accounting, which is why for audits tracking financial documents is critical. For auditors, ensuring a consistency of the data through proper sampling and testing is designed to reveal the kinds of problems that stem from improperly kept records — records that are more prone to errors in distributed networks.

I have shared these professional examples to show how important keeping good records is in a distributed network.

Of course, fixing the risks of record keeping in a distributed network is something that cloud computing was designed to do.

In cloud computing technology, people in different locations can edit documents that are updated in a shared location. But those documents are usually kept in a centralized location, and they do not always keep an easy-to-track record of who updated what and when. In some ways, this makes cloud computing like a centralized network, as in Figure 2-3, where all permissions and data are kept in one place. It also means that the network can be vulnerable to a central point of failure.

I will discuss the risks of central point of failure more in Chapter 3, but in short, it means that if you have all your records in one place, they are exposed. Similarly, if Dropbox or Google Drive stop working due to a technology problem, it also means that you may not be able to access your documents. And your system of documentation and record keeping will fail through no fault of your own, at least temporarily.

Figure 2-3: A Centralized Network

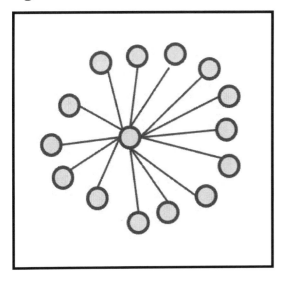

Better Than the Cloud

Blockchain technology is explicitly designed to allow people within a distributed system to receive updated ledgers of completed transactions. Think of it as a push system that constantly updates the network wherever its members are. Part of the reason that a blockchain can more consistently update a distributed network of entities is because the transactions are not centrally processed. They are processed by nodes within the network. This is shown in Figure 2-4.

Any node, or participant with permission, within the network of a blockchain can update the blockchain. But only one block can be added at a time. With Bitcoin, this is done through a process called mining, where rewards are given for completing complicated mathematical computations. The node that completes the transaction first wins an award, known as a redemption. Corporate blockchains can be structured to process transactions differently. In fact, blockchains are highly customizable.

Figure 2-4: Nodes in a Blockchain Network

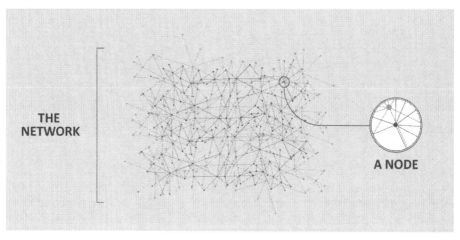

THE NETWORK

A NODE

Versatility of a Blockchain

As I've mentioned before, a blockchain is a kind of database technology. It is also an open source concept. This means that any entity creating a digital currency or corporate transaction-oriented blockchain can customize how the transactions are processed, what the rewards are, and the specifications for the process stack. Plus, the transactions can also be customized to include whatever details the creating entity would like added in order to ensure a complete set of records.

This also means that a blockchain does not need to be public.

For Bitcoin, you can download its blockchain. But as corporations consider creating their own blockchains, a topic I discuss further in Chapter 13, it is important to know that blockchains may be kept internally and shared among colleagues within an organization.

Of course, some of these may leak out, and we will discuss the cybersecurity implications of using a blockchain and increasing significantly the vulnerable attack surface or points of vulnerability in Chapter 16.

Use Cases and Tradeoffs

Blockchains have many uses, but these are the main structural points of a blockchains anatomy. Of course, as Melanie Swan has pointed out, blockchain "is not for every situation."[5] This is because processing blockchains can take a lot of time and energy. And there are tradeoffs between how public a blockchain is and how much security you need.

A large public blockchain, like Bitcoin, consumes vast amounts of energy. And over time, blockchains get larger and larger. After all, their ledgers are permanent. This risk that a blockchain will grow significantly in size is a concept known as bloat, and I will discuss it more thoroughly in Chapter 11.

For now, I want you to take away the following main points about the anatomy of a blockchain:

1. A blockchain has three parts: the record, the block, and the chain.
2. A blockchain has its greatest use case as a database management tool for distributed networks.
3. A blockchain is an efficient means of maintaining data in a distributed network because transactions are processed by nodes.
4. A blockchain has a reduced central point of failure.
5. A blockchain is not always the right choice for database management, and there are tradeoffs.

Now, let's talk about the greatest value of blockchain technology: reducing the risk of a central point of failure.

CHAPTER 3

CENTRAL POINT OF FAILURE

This is the chapter where we talk about the cover of this book.

I must admit that I wondered when I put this book together, if people would think I am opposed to blockchain, because the cover shows a fire.

But that isn't the case at all.

The cover of this book depicts the burning of the ancient Library of Alexandria — and the fire that consumed it. The central point of failure represented by the loss of the library is one of the greatest losses of knowledge in human history. And blockchain offers a counter to it, with its distributed ledger technology.

As a futurist, it is important to place technological developments in a historical context, and for me, the burning of the Library of Alexandria is essential for that context. You see, the Library of Alexandria was subject to a single point of failure. And a very specific kind of single point of failure — a central point of failure.

Single Point of Failure

The risk of a single point of failure is something that is often discussed in technology and supply chain circles. A single point of failure is when a network is exposed completely, but the weakness is at one point. If that one point fails, the entire network will fail.

An example of a single point of failure would be a transformer in a power grid that, if it fails, could cause the entire grid to go down. A technology example would be a router that, if it fails, eliminates internet access for a broader network of computers. In a global supply chain for a manufacturer, it may be that you have one vendor that makes a unique widget. And if that widget cannot be made, your entire business will seize up. You will no longer be able to manufacture your goods, your profits will fall, and your company could fail.

Any one thing that your business relies on as a choke point — or that you as an individual might rely on — could be considered a single point of failure. This is part of the reason that procurement professionals often consider these risks — and it's why networks have redundancies built into them to prevent broad systemic failures.

There are countless examples, and for a deeper discussion of the risks of a single point of failure, I would recommend the eponymous book on the subject, *Single Point of Failure*, by Gary Lynch.

Central Point of Failure

A central point of failure is a very specific kind of a single point of failure. A central point of failure threatens the existence of an entire system because of centralization. A centralized exposure and concentration in the system threatens the entire system.

A great example of a catastrophic central point of failure that greatly impacted documents and record keeping on a global scale was the burning of the ancient Library of Alexandria.

The Library of Alexandria

The last time you encountered the Library of Alexandria, or the similarly important Lighthouse of Alexandria, was playing some form of economic development game like Sid Meier's *Civilization*, in which you take a small village and build it up through the ages to become a modern civilization.

While the Lighthouse of Alexandria was one of the seven wonders of the ancient world as a lighthouse and beacon of light to ships traveling in the Mediterranean, it was the Library of Alexandria that was a real source of a more important kind of light, of illumination, and of knowledge.

The priceless treasure trove of documents amassed after Alexander the Great's death under the aegis of the Greek Ptolemaic dynasty of Pharos in Ancient Egypt was described as containing 500,000 scrolls.[2]

The Fire

Five hundred thousand scrolls of knowledge burned in the fire at the Library of Alexandria. All that knowledge, all that wisdom, all that information in one place at one time must have been amazing. And then they were gone.

Lost to the world forever.

This was perhaps the most costly central point of failure in the history of the world — the fire at the Library of Alexandria. It was a terrible loss in the ancient world.

And it was preventable.

Not in a Smokey the Bear kind of way that "only you, ancient Greeks, can prevent library fires." After all, Caesar was to blame, since the fire was a result of his seize of Alexandria and a fire that unintentionally spread to the library.[3] But the scale of the loss was preventable because the contents of the library were exposed to a central point of failure.

Despite all of the knowledge contained in the Library of Alexandria, one valuable, priceless lesson had to be learned — to forever serve as an example — that redundancies are critical for ensuring information is not lost.

It's widely reported that the books and records amassed at the Library of Alexandria were often copied, but the records at the library were largely originals. And many documents were unlikely to have been copied, given the time and cost.

Libraries Reduce Central Point of Failure Risks

The lesson of the Library of Alexandria was not lost on future record keepers, when throughout the Middle Ages monks tirelessly copied illuminated manuscripts by candlelight. Even today, and especially before the use of electronic documentation, redundancies of documentation among libraries has been critical. After all, the University of Virginia, where I went to college, is the backup book depository for the Library of Congress.

Today, many libraries tirelessly copy, convert, and distribute old documents into portable document files — or PDFs — in order to share information. But it also reduces central point of failure risk.

Corporations and Central Point of Failure Risks

When I worked on a trading desk as an economist at Wachovia Bank from 2004 to 2007, it was the third largest US bank at the time. We had a backup trading desk far away from Charlotte, which was the corporate headquarters.

This was something most banks and financial institutions created and maintained after the terrorist attacks in New York on 11 September 2001.

While some institutions and companies have learned to build redundancies into their systems, most entities are still exposed to a central point of failure.

And individuals are exposed, too.

Many people don't have backup copies of their work. The same is true of businesses. Nonprofits. Institutions.

Of course, the use of cloud computing has allowed people to share and back up their documents on Dropbox, Box, or Google Drive.

But that is also a central repository in some ways. There is a reliance on the cloud — something that could be subject to failure. If one of those entities should fail, it could be impactful in a very bad way — even if for only a short time.

Enter Blockchain

Reducing central point of failure risk is where blockchain comes in. Because while the cloud allows many people to access a single document, the blockchain allows for one document to be distributed among many through a network of nodes. And a permanent record of the most recent transaction is clear.

This improves version control, and it reduces the risk of a central point of failure.

There can be no Library of Alexandria that burns to the ground with all information lost, because the ledger of information on a blockchain is everywhere.

Essentially, your very own personal financial or corporate Library of Alexandria has cloned itself—and with a blockchain, it continually updates and redistributes itself to a network.

This is a core value proposition of blockchain: the ability to share and disseminate knowledge in a way that provides consistent, distributed redundancy of information. It is one of the main value propositions of blockchain, but it is often one of the most overlooked values.

So, is blockchain the hope that prevents a future Library of Alexandria-level loss of information, of institutional knowledge, of wisdom? I believe it is.

This is the greatest promise of blockchain.

Figure 3-1: The Library of Alexandria[4]

CHAPTER 4

THE ORIGINS OF BLOCKCHAIN AND BITCOIN

The creator of the blockchain and Bitcoin is Satoshi Nakamoto.

Who is Satoshi? No one knows.

It is widely speculated that Satoshi is not the real name of the person who created Bitcoin and proposed the concept of a blockchain. In fact, many people think that Satoshi is not an individual at all, but rather a group of people.

Satoshi published a white paper titled "Bitcoin: A Peer-to-Peer Electronic Cash System" on 31 October 2008.[1] This paper presented the idea of engaging in making financial payments electronically, without the use of a financial institution or intermediary. As the title of the paper indicates, it discusses the nature of a proposed electronic cash system in which peers interact directly making non-reversible, peer-to-peer transactions.

This theoretical paper was followed up by the first transaction in Bitcoin on 3 January 2009.

And thus, Bitcoin was created out of nothing. Backed by nothing. There is no central bank, no government, and no foreign currency reserves. And it used a blockchain as a means of keeping a permanent public ledger of all future Bitcoin transactions.

Blockchain as Combustion Engine

The use of a blockchain was a theoretical concept until the first Bitcoin transaction occurred. It has become intertwined with Bitcoin in the same way that the combustion engine, which was invented in 1885, is intertwined with our idea of cars and trucks.[2]

But Bitcoin is not blockchain, and blockchain is not Bitcoin.

Blockchain is the technology engine that powers Bitcoin, but blockchain can power many things.

Blockchain can improve transparency of goods transport and freight. And it can allow for greater ease in transactions that rely on antiquated documentation processes in industries that are ripe for disruption. It can protect people from unsafe agricultural products, while also preventing losses in foodstuffs that are similar — but from safe sources. And it can allow for easier financial recordkeeping and potentially for the transfer of medical records. I will discuss these topics in Chapters 14 and 15.

But while blockchain can do those great things, it can also be used by criminals, terrorists, and subversive political actors who seek to use the anonymity of Bitcoin and cryptocurrencies to do bad things.

Blockchain is like the combustion engine, which can power a number of vehicles — from the engine of a kamikaze submarine, a coast guard rescue cutter, or a Disney cruise ship. The blockchain engine has so many uses. But while some of them are bad, many of them are good.

And in the same way that people don't think about the explosions in their car engine — which is the definition of combustion — the explosions are occurring nonetheless.

And the biggest explosions of blockchain are likely to be disruptive to industries that are plagued by documentation issues, inefficiencies of information, and ownership transfers. These areas with large addressable markets for blockchain solutions present the opportunity for a sizable return on investment for blockchain solutions.

Figure 4-1: A Combustion Engine[3]

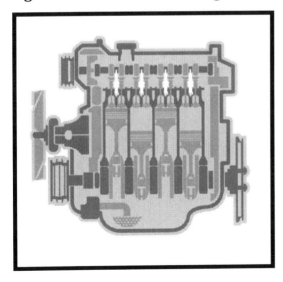

Blockchain and Bitcoin

The origin of Bitcoin is backed by both financial and theoretical logic. And while Bitcoin and cryptocurrencies have significant value propositions and use cases, blockchain is likely to outgrow Bitcoin and cryptocurrencies.

It will have many other high-value uses in the same way that the vehicles that use combustion engines today are far more advanced than the ones in which they were first used.

CHAPTER 5

THE ECONOMICS OF CRYPTO

The economics that support the use and value of cryptocurrencies, including Bitcoin, are rooted in concerns about fiat currencies and the policies of central banks.

Of course, part of the historical and theoretical libertarian argument for non-government currencies also stemmed from a distrust of fiat currencies. I will discuss this further in Chapter 6. In this chapter, I focus on the economics of Bitcoin and other digital currencies against a backdrop of concern about the future of fiat currencies and central bank policies.

One of the biggest challenges in the wake of the financial crisis was how to stimulate economic growth at a time of almost unprecedented slowing. Expanding central bank balance sheets was one of the unprecedented critical solutions that the US Federal Reserve, the Bank of England, the European Central Bank, the Bank of Japan, and other central banks took to keep their economies afloat.

This is one of the things that prompted Satoshi Nakamoto's white paper and the introduction of Bitcoin — at least based on the message included with the first Bitcoin transaction.

This first Bitcoin transaction is often referred to as the Genesis Block, which included the following message:

The Times 03/Jan/2009 Chancellor on brink of second bailout for banks[1]

The Bank of England engaged in multiple bailouts and a 300 percent expansion in the size of its balance sheet between 2007 and 2012, from around 94 billion British pounds to over 400 billion, as you can see in Figure 5-1.

Figure 5-1: Bank of England Balance Sheet[2]

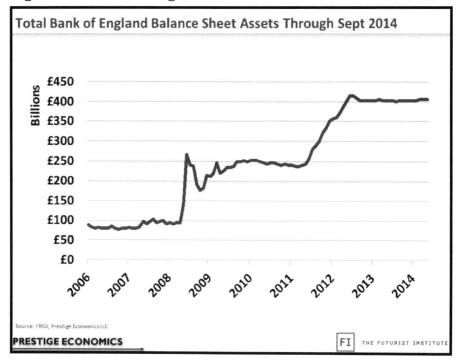

But the Bank of England was not alone in taking these kinds of measures. The European Central Bank also increased its balance sheet massively. The ECB expanded its balance sheet from 1.3 trillion euros in January 2008 to 3.1 trillion euros in June 2012. Then, from June 2012 until September 2014, the ECB reduced its balance sheet by about one-third — letting it fall from 3.1 trillion euros to 2.0 trillion euros.

During that time, however, the Eurozone economy slowed and the Eurozone manufacturing PMI also conveyed a significant slowdown. The risk of a triple-dip recession in the Eurozone increased. As a result of this sharp slowdown, the ECB switched gears and rapidly expanded its balance sheet, which rose to over 4.6 trillion euros by July 2018.

Figure 5-2: European Central Bank Balance Sheet[3]

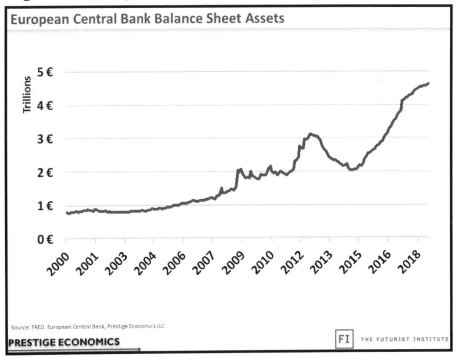

Source: FRED, European Central Bank, Prestige Economics LLC

PRESTIGE ECONOMICS

FI   THE FUTURIST INSTITUTE

The expansion of a central bank balance sheets was enacted as an extreme means to lower interest rates and indirectly stimulate financial activity and economic growth. This was achieved by having a central bank engage in buying government debt, mortgages, bonds, or equities. Each major central bank took a slightly different approach.

The most aggressive central bank expansion was implemented by the Bank of Japan, the quantitative easing program of which has included significant purchases of Japanese real estate investment trusts, known as J-REITs, as well as exchange-traded funds or ETFs of Japanese equities. In other words, the Bank of Japan has been a big buyer of Japanese equities.

Figure 5-3: Bank of Japan Balance Sheet[4]

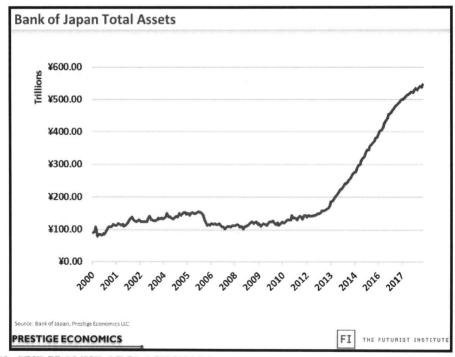

In 2010, the Bank of Japan did not own any ETFs, but by March 2011, the BoJ's ownership of ETFs had increased to 185 billion Japanese yen. By September 2016, it had risen to 9.8 trillion JPY. Currently, the Bank of Japan owns about 16 trillion JPY worth of ETFs. And the BoJ is a major shareholder of many equities.

This situation is unprecedented and precarious, and it forces us to ask some difficult questions: How will the Bank of Japan disentangle itself from Japanese equity markets? Will the BoJ ever be able to sell its equities? Will other central banks get themselves into a similar pickle? It is difficult to predict what will happen to Japanese equity markets if the BoJ steps back. But it does seem likely that other central banks could go down this path. And that risk is supportive of cryptocurrencies.

Figure 5-4: BoJ Balance Sheet ETF Holdings[5]

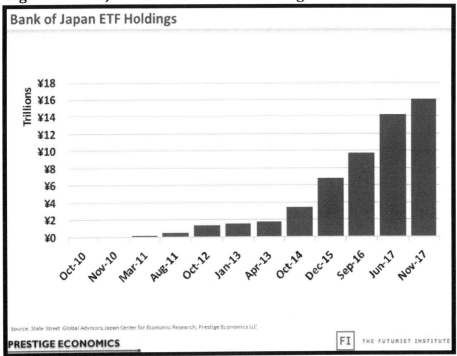

The Federal Reserve

In response to slow growth after the Great Recession, the US Federal Reserve engaged in purchasing mortgage-backed securities as a means to push down mortgage rates and stimulate housing activity in the United States. The Fed also purchased Treasuries, which pushed down interest rates — even after the federal funds rate was set by the Federal Reserve at zero percent.

The Fed increased its balance sheet in 2008 from around 900 billion dollars in January 2008 to around a peak of 4.5 trillion dollars by January 2015. But it did not buy equities or corporate bonds, although that is something that it may consider doing in the future. Presently, however, the Fed is focused on reducing the level of its balance sheet. But in the future, it may also consider buying equities or corporate bonds.

Figure 5-5: Total Fed Balance Sheet Assets[6]

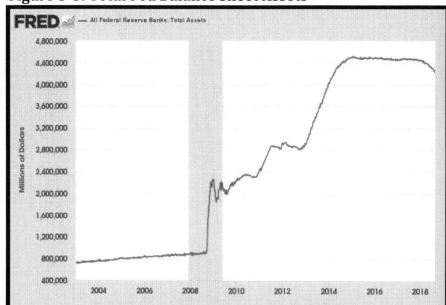

Beginning in October 2017, the US Fed began reducing its balance sheet in a formal policy of balance sheet reductions by reducing reinvestment of expiring mortgage-backed securities and Treasuries. Unlike the European Central Bank's attempt to reduce its balance sheet, however, the Fed has deliberately planned a very slow pace of balance sheet reductions. It was, I believe, in part due to the experience of the ECB that the Fed decided to be especially cautious.

The Future of Quantitative Easing

Even though the Fed is reducing its balance sheet, the balance sheet is likely to remain at or near historic levels for a very long time to come. And it is likely to expand further in the future — rather than see declines down to levels seen before the Great Recession that lasted from December 2007 to June 2009.

Expanding the Fed's balance sheet was highly effective at stimulating the US economy. In other words, quantitative easing works. This means that the Fed is likely to expand its balance sheet again in the future.

Furthermore, Janet Yellen noted at the annual Kansas City Fed event at Jackson Hole, Wyoming in 2016 that "I expect that forward guidance and asset purchases will remain important components of the Fed's policy toolkit." She further added that "Future policymakers may wish to explore the possibility of purchasing a broader range of assets."[7]

In other words, the Fed is not just likely to engage in quantitative easing again in the future, but the Fed is likely to buy different kinds of securities in the future as well. So, while Fed policy could get tighter before it gets looser, it is likely to get much looser in the future.

This expansion of central bank balance sheets is fundamentally supportive of the economic and financial argument in favor of Bitcoin and digital currencies that are not backed by central banks. The impact of the expansions and persistently high levels of central bank balance sheets of the ECB and the Bank of England is unclear.

What is clear, however, is that central banks have cracked open the QE cookie jar — and that they are likely to spend more money they don't have, effectively creating the ability to purchase assets out of thin air. There is no problem, from an accounting standpoint, if the assets eventually expire in value and fall off the balance sheet. But that is not going to be the case with the balance sheet of the Bank of Japan.

And then there is the issue of debt.

The National Debt

Aside from the Fed's rising balance sheet, the US national debt is a growing problem. At almost $21.4 trillion in August 2018, the national debt is not a small sum. In fact, it comes out to almost $65,200 for every US citizen — every man, woman, and child.[8]

That is a lot of debt!

Figure 5-6: Total US Federal Debt[9]

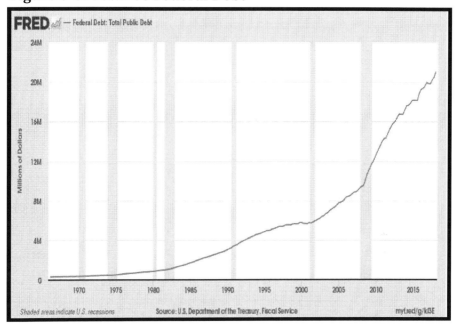

Figure 5-7: Total Federal Debt as a Percent of GDP[10]

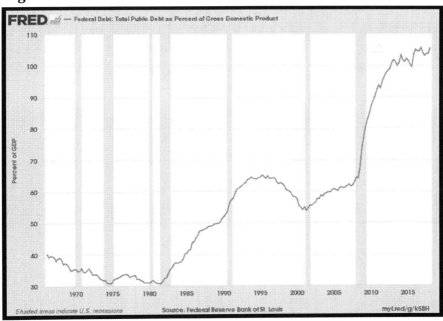

In the event of a future US recession, the US debt level and the ratio of debt to GDP will rise. But even without a recession, the level of the national debt and the national debt as a percent of GDP, which are shown in Figures 5-6 and 5-7, are likely to rise significantly in coming years.

And entitlements are a major source of additional imminent debt.

Unfortunately, while the US national debt is large, the unfunded financial obligations stemming from US entitlements are much larger — and they are likely to compound US debt problems in coming years. Simply put, entitlements pose the greatest threat to future US government debt levels — and US economic growth.

Entitlements

US entitlements, including Medicare, Medicaid, and Social Security, are financed by payroll taxes from workers. Payroll taxes are separate from income taxes, and while income tax rates could fall if fiscal policies change, payroll taxes are on a one-way trip higher. You see, entitlements are wildly underfunded.

All the sovereign debt in the world totals around $60 trillion. [11] That is the debt cumulatively held by all national governments in the world. But the size of unfunded US entitlements might be more than three times that level. That's right: the unfunded, off-balance-sheet obligations for Medicare, Medicaid, and Social Security could be $200 trillion.[12]

This level of off-balance-sheet debt obligation existentially threatens the US economy.

The Heritage Foundation has taken calculations from the US Congressional Budget Office about entitlements to create Figure 5-8, which looks quite catastrophic. Basically, by 2030, all US tax revenue will be consumed by entitlements and the interest on the national debt. And these were the dismal calculations before tax reform and the most recent US budget threatened to increase the national debt further.

The year 2030 is not that far in the future, and the clock is ticking.

But despite the magnitude of the entitlements problem, do not expect this to be an issue that will be addressed any time soon. This willful ignorance of the political powers that be for mounting debt presents support for crypto.

Figure 5-8: Tax Revenue Spent on Entitlements[13]

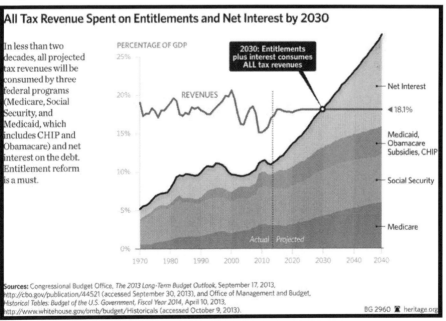

All Tax Revenue Spent on Entitlements and Net Interest by 2030

In less than two decades, all projected tax revenues will be consumed by three federal programs (Medicare, Social Security, and Medicaid, which includes CHIP and Obamacare) and net interest on the debt. Entitlement reform is a must.

2030: Entitlements plus interest consumes ALL tax revenues

Net Interest
◀ 18.1%
Medicaid, Obamacare Subsidies, CHIP
Social Security
Medicare

Actual | Projected

Sources: Congressional Budget Office, The 2013 Long-Term Budget Outlook, September 17, 2013, http://cbo.gov/publication/44521 (accessed September 30, 2013), and Office of Management and Budget, Historical Tables: Budget of the U.S. Government, Fiscal Year 2014, April 10, 2013, http://www.whitehouse.gov/omb/budget/Historicals (accessed October 9, 2013).

BG 2960 ☎ heritage.org

The Grandfather of US Social Security

Part of the problem with entitlements stems from their origins. The US Social Security Administration website credits Otto von Bismarck as the grandfather of US entitlements. Bismarck's portrait is even on the US Social Security Administration's website (Figure 5-9).

Bismarck was a powerful politician known for his use of *Realpolitik*, a political doctrine built on pragmatism to advance national self-interests. For him, entitlements were convenient and expedient. Unfortunately, that is no longer the case. Today, entitlements threaten to crush the US economy with increased levels of debt. And without reform, they could decimate the US workforce.

Figure 5-9: Grandfather of Social Security, Otto von Bismarck[14]

Bismarck's system was also sustainable. His system guaranteed a pension to German workers over 70, but the average life expectancy in Germany in the late 1880s was only 40.[15] In other words, so few people were expected to receive the benefits that the program's cost would be negligible.

Bismarck rigged entitlements to help crush his political opponents, without having to pay out. But the current entitlement system in the United States is an unfunded liability that threatens to crush the entire economy and usher in a labor market Robocalypse. Plus, fixing entitlements presents a horrible dilemma as many Americans rely heavily on entitlements for income (Figure 5-10).

Figure 5-10: Expected Importance of Social Security[16]

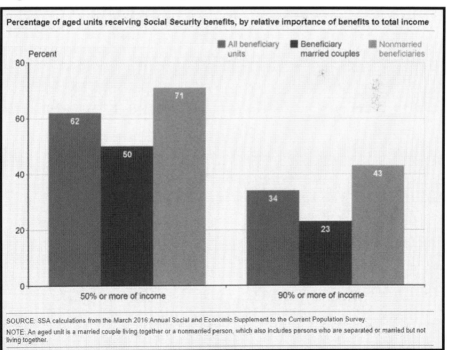

But how did this system break down? Bismarck had such a good thing going. What happened?

This can be answered in one word: demographics.

Demographics

US population growth has slowed sharply, and this demographic shift appears unstoppable. Plus, as birthrates have fallen, life expectancy has also risen. This compounds the funding shortfalls for entitlements.

Population growth in the United States has fallen from annual rates of over 1.5 percent per year during the 1950s and early 1960s to just 0.7 percent since 2011.[17] Some of this slowing in population growth is due to a decline in the US fertility rate. In general, fertility rates have been dropping globally, but according to demographer Jonathan Last, the US fertility rate is still relatively high at 1.93.[18] The US total fertility rate is relatively high compared to other industrialized nations, but it is below the 2.1 percent "golden number," which is required to maintain a population, according to Last.[19]

Without enough people paying into Social Security and entitlements, the system is at increased risk of failure. And the discussion of entitlements is another likely reason people may find value in digital currencies.

Future Implications

While the prospects of higher US debt levels in the future are almost guaranteed, this increases the chance that the US central bank — the Federal Reserve — will need to expand its balance sheet further, in order to keep interest rates low. Without low interest rates, the US government could face an even more rapidly rising interest rate burden — a burden that existentially threatens the US economy.

In general, the various government bailouts and central bank balance sheet expansions that followed the financial crisis and the Great Recession of 2007 to 2009 highlighted the potential for governments and central banks — the guardians of fiat currency value, government budgets, and the public trust — to acquiesce when big entities at risk of failure could have engendered systemic breakdowns. This led to the designation of some companies and firms as "too big to fail."

It is against this backdrop of central bank bailouts and quantitative easing that Bitcoin was born. And these risks continue to support the economic argument for cryptocurrencies.

We currently live in a time of rising uncertainty for the future path of central bank policies and government budgets. And it is a time where the economic and theoretical arguments for non-government-backed fiat currency are likely to continue to seem reasonable.

CHAPTER 6

HAYEK DREAMS OF BITCOIN

As an economist, I wonder if Austrian economist F. A. Hayek would have dreamt of Bitcoins. After all, there is an entire body of economic theory that supports the notion of currency outside of governments.

Hayek was a free-market economist who was well known for criticizing the monetary system we have, in which there is a government monopoly over the issuance of currency. While other Austrian economists have, at times, favored a return to the gold standard, Hayek noted there are problems with that plan.

For example: there isn't enough gold to transact on. This is part of the reason that currencies became fiat in the first place. The dollar became the global reserve currency, in part, because there are enough dollars out there to facilitate transactions. Of course, gold prices have trended higher in dollar terms since the end of the Bretton Woods system in the 1970s.

For Hayek, a return to the gold standard would be unreasonable, because it "would probably lead to such a rise (and perhaps also violent fluctuations) of the price of gold that, though it might still be used widely for hoarding, it would soon cease to be convenient as the unit for business transactions and accounting."[1]

In other words, while using gold as a medium of exchange would limit currency devaluation potential, just announcing that it would be the benchmark could make it unreasonably priced. Hayek was quick to point out that "we certainly can do better than [the gold standard], though not through government."[2] And this is where Bitcoin comes in.

Figure 6-1: Nominal Monthly Price of Gold[3]

Gold Prices

Gold prices have generally trended higher since the end of Bretton Woods in the early 1970s.

Gold prices spiked during the global financial crisis but subsequently fell when the dollar strengthened during the period following the European sovereign debt crisis. At the time this book was written, the price of gold had been trending higher since early 2016, but it remained sharply lower than during 2011 and 2012.

As opposed to turning to gold, in the late 1970s, Hayek explicitly advocated for privately created currencies to replace government -issued currencies: "We would get for the first time a money where the whole business of issuing money could be effected only by the issuer issuing good money"4 Of course, blockchain technology and Bitcoin did not exist in the late 1970s.

Personal computers barely existed!

But, Bitcoin *could* fit the bill — as might other blockchain-supported digital currencies. As such, it is possible people will turn more seriously to these digital currencies, if public trust in the safety and surety of their monetary value can be secured. This is a critical challenge for Bitcoin, because its wallets have been hacked in the past, causing a rapid loss of confidence — and value. And there are also regulatory challenges related to Bitcoin regulation.

I discuss these dynamics more in Chapter 16.

As with all markets, there are two factors that have been driving Bitcoin prices: supply and demand. The analysis below comes from work I wrote in September 2016 as part of the MIT FinTech certificate course I completed.

Demand for Digital Currencies

We live in an uncertain era of unprecedented central bank quantitative easing that has engendered a ballooning of central bank balance sheets. If concern about these — and future — central bank policies increases, then Bitcoin and other digital cryptocurrencies, along with the blockchain technology that enables them, are likely to offer investors, consumers, and individuals alternatives to government-produced currencies. Instead of gold being viewed as the only potential store of value (which is unreasonable, because using gold as a currency would only make its value spike, thus making it inviable as a currency alternative), these private currencies could offer the public an alternative. The low transaction costs of digital currencies, and their existence outside of banking, could make them increasingly attractive for use in transactions, as the means of hedging currency risk, and as investment vehicles.

Supply of Digital Currencies

The trick to preserving the value of Bitcoin and other digital currencies will lie with the restriction of the monetary supply. Bitcoin is created through an award process, known as mining, which is tied to the processing of Bitcoin payment transactions. This is very different than the creation of a government-backed currency that simply prints more of the currency it uses at will.

For Bitcoin and other digital currencies, if the supply can be limited in such a way as to avoid devaluation, it would fulfill Hayek's dreams — and further disrupt the government-controlled system of fiat currencies.

That is something Bitcoin actively did in 2016, by reducing the payout to miners by 50 percent. This proved to be an important contributing factor to the significant rise in Bitcoin's value throughout 2017.

The future of Bitcoin will hinge less on theory and more on security and regulation. But in a post-Bretton Woods world and an era of unprecedented quantitative easing, the theoretical justification for Bitcoin and cryptocurrencies seems more valid than ever. And while some regulators may have nightmares about cryptocurrencies, Hayek may very well have dreamt of them.

CHAPTER 7

OTHER CRYPTOCURRENCIES AND INITIAL COIN OFFERINGS

Bitcoin isn't the only digital currency — or cryptocurrency — out there. There are a number of major cryptos, including Ethereum, Litecoin, Ripple, and a rapidly growing number of others. Many of these currencies have been created through initial coin offerings — or ICOs.

Of course, the concept of currencies outside the control of governments is not new. Aside from the concepts postulated by Hayek in the 1970s, I was exposed to a more recent example before the cryptomania of 2017 and 2018 — in 2009, not long after Bitcoin was introduced.

Back in November 2009, the European Journalism Centre hosted an event in Brussels called Covering the Crisis. The event was focused on understanding what conditions led to the global financial crisis — and how the media was behind the curve, missing the greatest global economic crisis since the Great Depression. I attended this event as a speaker, and I gave a talk titled "The Story Not Reported." I also sat on a panel about who controls media messaging.

It was an insightful event, and it wasn't my speech that was the most interesting and left tongues wagging. It was a talk by Bernard Lietaer, a Research Fellow at the Center for Sustainable Resources at the University of California at Berkeley. His talk was titled "Questioning the Paradigm of Money."[1] It was focused on complimentary currencies.

Lietaer described complementary currencies as currencies that operate "parallel with conventional money, are useful at all times for social issues, for economic issues."[2] He discussed how these complimentary currencies were being used at the very local level in Uruguay and Brazil.

This talk was given just over 10 months after the Genesis Block of Bitcoin had been issued. And it blew the minds of the attendees.

The group of economists, senior journalists, policymakers, and financial thought leaders found it very difficult to believe that money outside of the global financial system would work, even though the global financial system was failing — and the global economy was under tremendous pressure.

My talk and this talk on money were published after the conference in an eponymous book titled *Covering the Crisis: The Role of the Media in the Financial Crisis*.[3] It is just as valuable for consideration today as it was in 2009.

As one of the world's top-ranked currency forecasters, I was — and remain — intrigued by Lietaer's comments. They have stayed with me.

The distrust in financial institutions, especially central banks, has not abated. And the economic fundamentals I discussed in Chapter 5 that partially justify concerns about central banks and our current financial system have strengthened. In truth, the significant economic hangover from the global financial crisis and the accompanying unprecedented, broad-based skepticism about the nature of the global financial system has contributed to the gradual increase in interest in Bitcoin and alternative currencies outside the current system.

Altcoins

Cryptocurrencies other than Bitcoin are often called *altcoins*. And as Bitcoin prices began to rise, as in Figure 7-1, the number of altcoins has increased.

Figure 7-1: Price of Bitcoin[4]

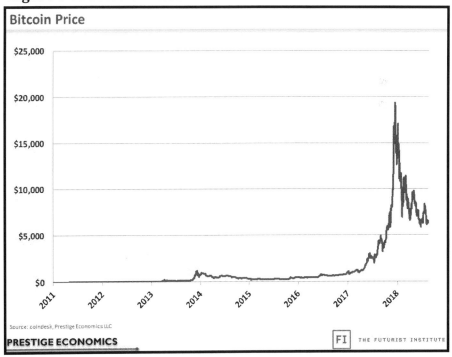

Some of the most widely discussed altcoins are Ethereum, which was created in 2014; Ripple, which was initially released in 2012, and Litecoin; which was created in 2011.

Of these, Ethereum and Ripple are perhaps the two most interesting, in my opinion. Ethereum is the most critical, but we will take a look at Ripple later in this chapter.

Ethereum is interesting because it operates as a platform on which other coins can be created. When I think of Bitcoin versus Ethereum, it makes me think about the battle between the video cassette technologies of Betamax and VHS in the late 1970s and 1980s.[5]

VHS won that battle — even though Betamax was the superior technology. The reason VHS won is because the technology was allowed to be licensed broadly.

In the battle between Bitcoin versus Ethereum, Bitcoin is the Betamax — it is its own thing to the extent that anything other than Bitcoin is considered an altcoin — an *alt*ernative to Bitcoin, which has been seen as the leading cryptocurrency.

But it is Ethereum, which functions as VHS did in the video cassette wars. It is relatively easy to create new coins and tokens using an Ethereum platform. This has increased the demand for Ethereum, and it has led to the propagation of countless other coins, which are usually issued through a process called an ICO — or an Initial Coin Offering.

Initial Coin Offerings—ICOs

Most cryptocurrencies, altcoins, and ICOs start the same way Bitcoin did. In fact, there is even a widely distributed meme of an ICO roadmap that often appears online — and that you can see below in Figure 7-2.

The ICO process starts a with an **idea**, which leads to **research**. After the research comes a **white paper** — like the kind Satoshi wrote about Bitcoin. And then comes the **ICO launch**.

And believe me, many people expect these to be launches!

In essence, ICOs are like Initial Public Offerings for small companies — for startups. Many ICOs have shown significantly outsized financial returns. For this reason, many investors expect that ICOs will continue to yield outsized returns.

This is where one of the most well-known concepts of the ICO launch has been turned into a meme — a kind of visual joke — about ICOs called "When Moon? When Lambo?"

Figure 7-2: ICO Roadmap[6]

Established ICO Roadmap

① Idea ② Research ③ Whitepaper ④ ICO Launch

When Moon? When Lambo?

The questions "When Moon? When Lambo?" from hopeful investors about an ICO are more fully explained as meaning:

When will the value of this ICO go to the moon?

When can I buy a Lamborghini with my modest investment?

There is often a debate among cryptoenthusiasts — people who are big fans of cryptocurrencies — about how much "When moon?" means, but a 10,000% percent return is often cited.

With such massive potential returns, and so much money in play, ICOs ramped up in 2017 to record levels, as seen in Figure 7-3.

Figure 7-3: Number of Initial Coin Offerings[7]

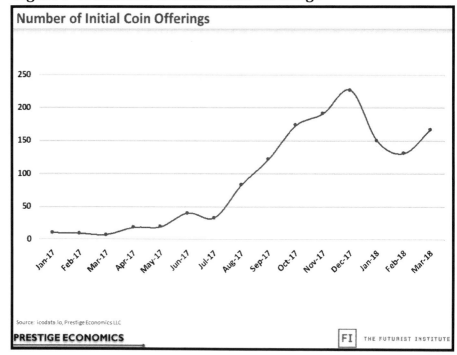

Number of Initial Coin Offerings

Source: icodata.io, Prestige Economics LLC

PRESTIGE ECONOMICS   FI   THE FUTURIST INSTITUTE

As I mentioned above, part of the reason for the rise in the number of ICOs and the value created in ICOs has been tied to the price of Bitcoin, as can be seen in Figure 7-4.

Needless to say, investments that present such outsized returns as a 10,000% ROI also present massive risks. I will discuss some of the potentially risky dynamics of investing in Bitcoin, altcoins, blockchain, and ICOs in Chapter 15.

The biggest risk in the immediate term is the change in regulatory environments that could affect how Bitcoin and altcoins are used — and who can participate in an ICO. In 2017, there were already prohibitions in place against marketing ICOs to Americans.

Figure 7-4: Number of Initial Coin Offerings[8]

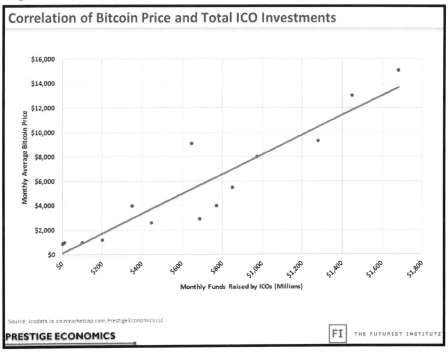

Utility Tokens and Coins

There are two main things that an ICO can do. First, it can involve the creation of a new cryptocurrency, which is explicitly designed as a security and its sole purpose is for trading. This is the purpose of Bitcoin, Ethereum, Litecoin, and many other altcoins.

But there is also a second thing that an ICO can do: it can allow a company to issue tokens or coins that can be used at some time in the future as part of a business enterprise. These are called utility tokens. Although they are intended to be used on a platform, they are often traded as securities — and the platforms may never come to fruition.

ICOs raised significant funds in 2017 and 2018, with the average monthly amounts shown in Figure 7-5. You can also see the total funds raised by all ICOs in Figure 7-6, which shows a peak coinciding with Bitcoin's price peak in December 2017.

ICO Seigniorage

Before I delve into the regulatory risks and trading risks associated with ICOs, I want to share a couple analogies about ICOs. You see, the notion of creating a currency that people might not actually spend is not new.

Economists call this seigniorage. A mentor of mine once described it as the ability of some countries to print money, and in exchange for that printed money, other countries would send them stuff. This is basically what happens to all reserve currencies, like the US dollar, the Japanese yen, the euro, and the British pound.

Figure 7-5: Average Amount Raised by ICOs[9]

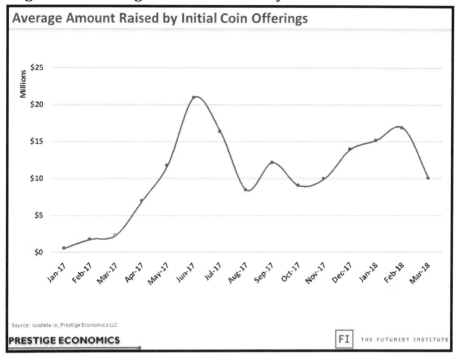

Figure 7-6: Total Funds Raised by ICOs[10]

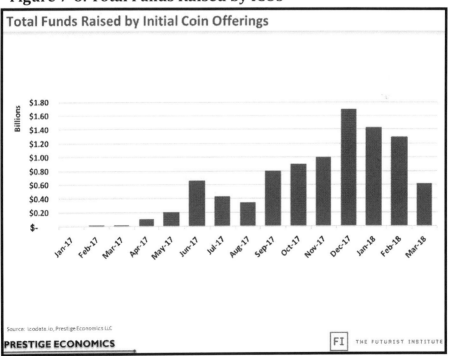

Essentially, countries keep the printed currency in their central bank reserves — locked in vaults — and they never use them. But the trick is: the country that printed the money got something in exchange.

And a similar thing happens with ICOs.

These tokens or coins are created out of nothing — often using the Ethereum platform — and then people buy them, trade them, and horde them.

Let's consider an example: Imagine there is a company that is planning to create an artificial intelligence résumé writer. It might issue an ICO with utility tokens that would eventually be used to pay for the AI résumé writer to write your résumé. Of course, the résumé writer would not need to exist at the time of the ICO, but the token or coin would only be usable — would only have real utility — on that not-as-yet existing platform. After all, the ICO comes before the launch — and before the company is usually operating. This is how ICOs are like crowdfunding.

An Extension of Crowdfunding
When the US JOBS Act was passed in 2012, it also included provisions for 200 million people — i.e. everyone in the United States over the age of 18 — to invest in private companies.

Private companies are those that you or I might start, but they could also become big. At the time this book went to print in August 2018, there were dozens of private companies worth billions of dollars.

This includes private startups like Uber, Lyft, and SpaceX, but it also includes well-established firms like Samsung, Deloitte, Bosch, Cargill, and IKEA.

Of course, the JOBS Act wasn't designed to help IKEA and Uber get more funding. It was focused on supporting funding for small entities. And this equity funding would come from the crowd — hence the term *equity crowdfunding*. It is also called *crowdequity*.

Historically, investments in private companies have been viewed as highly speculative. As such, it was not something the average investor could do. It just wasn't safe. But then along came crowdfunding platforms like Indiegogo and Kickstarter, which allowed business owners to raise funds for projects with a future hope of a reward.

Crowdfunding extended from group funding of what were initially gimmicky arts and crafts projects and geeky tech items that might otherwise have been found on quirky online websites — or in the now defunct *SkyMall* magazine — into *crowdequity* and *crowdlending* "investment" opportunities.

One big risk with these areas is that they have never seen a downturn. And in tough economic times, the crowd can vanish quickly. But that hasn't been the biggest risk for crowdequity owners so far. In truth, it is the illiquidity of investments in small private entities that is a bigger problem,

You see, crowdequity owners are required by the JOBS Act to hold their equities for a year before they can sell.

And this is where the ICO tokens come in. Since the JOBS Act prevented an exit from equity crowdfunding investments, investors found a new way to get more rapid liquidity: ICO tokens and coins. By investing in an ICO, there is likely to be liquidity — or at least more liquidity than for an investment with a mandatory one-year holding period.

Tech fever mixed with equity crowdfunding, as well as the anonymity and newness of blockchain, fed into ICO fever. And it has fueled massive interest in very speculative investments.

Disney Dollars

Another way to think about ICOs is to consider Disney Dollars.

Throughout the 1980s and 1990s, you could go to Walt Disney World, Disneyland, or a Disney Store and buy Disney Dollars. This was a company-created currency that had cute pictures of Mickey and Minnie Mouse on them. Some had Goofy. Some had Donald Duck. But they would be exchanged for real dollars. And you could only use them one place — at a Disney entity.

They had a fixed exchange rate — 1 US Dollar per 1 Disney Dollar. And many people kept them as souvenirs. In truth, they were competing with mall and other gift certificates, which in the 1980s and 1990s were still printed on pieces of paper.

Essentially, Disney was able to engage in seigniorage. Disney would print these cartoon dollars, and people would give them real US dollars in exchange. But many people would never spend the Disney Dollars.

They were a kind of souvenir. And Disney would never have to deliver on any products when the Disney Dollars would be redeemed, because in all likelihood, they would not be.

ICOs are kind of like those Disney Dollars, except instead of a Fortune 100 company with a number of theme parks and stores where you could spend your Disney Dollars, many companies with ICOs would never, ever create anything.

Essentially, investors might be buying Disney Dollars for Disney Worlds that will never be created.

Groupon

One further way to consider ICOs, especially in light of the Disney Dollar analogy, is that they are kind of like Groupons for stores that may never be built.

Groupons are a kind of pre-paid coupon — like a gift certificate — that became popular in the 2000s and 2010s. ICO coins and utility tokens, as an extension of crowdfunding, can also be considered similar to Groupons.

The big difference, of course, is that the company may never come to fruition. This is especially true with the prospects of additional regulation. You may not be able to trade those tokens and coins at some point.

Then, you would be stuck with the 2010s equivalent of a digital Blockbuster gift card.

As I will discuss further in Chapter 16, there are significant risks to investing in ICOs and cryptocurrencies. And there is a shifting regulatory framework, which is designed to initiate greater levels of visibility and control to crowd out fraudulent, illegal, and other subversive activities that are being financed by coin and token trading. This will be significantly impactful for the future of these investments.

Changes in Regulation Matter

The changes in US and global regulatory frameworks and guidance significantly impacted the pace and value of ICOs in 2018. In Figures 7-5 and 7-6, you can see how strong ICOs were in 2017, but that there was a sharp slowdown in 2018.

In a span of just a few months, financial institutions, banks, and credit card companies refused to allow their credit cards to be used to purchase Bitcoin and other cyrptocurrencies. Even Facebook and Google banned cryptocurrency and Bitcoin ads.

Even I was working on an ICO in 2017, but the rapidly changing regulatory environment in July and August of 2017 killed the deal. While the project I was working on had a team trying to create a high-value chatbot and artificial intelligence project, not all ICOs were or are valuable.

In fact, ICOs have been the source of many scams. And there are no guarantees that an ICO that receives funding will actually do *anything* at all.

These risks are significant, and the massive number of scams in the ICO space has led to the creation of another visual joke — another meme. It's what I call the "ICO Roadmap of Doom," and you can see it in Figure 7-7. In this figure, the ICO starts off normally, with an idea, research, white paper, and launch. But because of the dishonest or fraudulent nature of the project, it quickly turns to SEC and legal consequences.

Figure 7-7: ICO Roadmap of Doom[11]

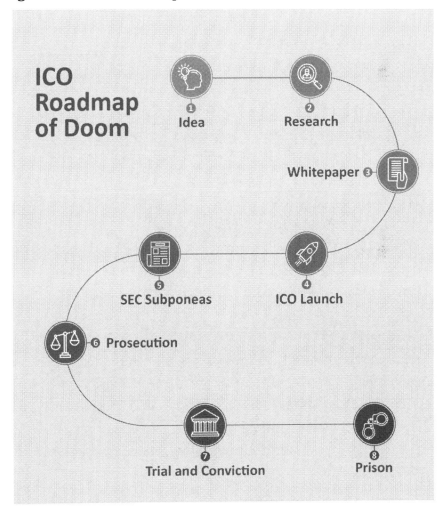

Ripple

Earlier in this chapter, I mentioned that there are two major cryptocurrencies that interested me. And while I have spent a great deal of time talking about Ethereum, ICOs, and fringe cryptocurrency activities, we need to discuss Ripple — one of the coins looking to operate within the current financial system and its regulatory framework.

Unlike Bitcoin and Ethereum, which seek to operate outside the current financial system, Ripple is interesting because it seeks to operate within the SWIFT international banking system as a means to improve foreign exchange transactions.

I probably find this concept very interesting, because it was the focus of a startup I created when I was studying FinTech at MIT in 2016. The company I created, called Hedgefly, used Bitcoin and its blockchain technology foundation on the backend to reduce future foreign exchange risk for travelers. As someone who travels internationally for work a lot, I wanted to solve a problem I faced regularly — relatively high FX transaction costs for individuals and small and medium-sized enterprises (SMEs). And what started as a class project turned into a real company.

Unfortunately, as Bitcoin volatility massively surpassed foreign exchange rate volatility of most major currencies, it was no longer a viable means of managing and reducing FX risk across currencies. Plus, other solutions came into prominence. But where Hedgefly failed, Ripple has taken the lead in pushing for a disruption of the inefficient and expensive international FX payments market.

CHAPTER 8

BOHEMIAN BITCOIN

On a certain day in early August 2018, I found myself in the Czech Republic — in Bohemia. Much to the occasional chagrin of my very tolerant and loving wife, I occasionally check my Twitter and LinkedIn feeds when I am on vacation. And on this one particular day in Bohemia, I saw two stories.

The first post in my feed is from a good friend, and newly appointed deputy Vice Chairman of the New York Stock Exchange (NYSE), with an article about how the NYSE wants to make Bitcoin legit and available to everyone's 401K.

The second is a post noting that Goldman says the value of Bitcoin will fall.

As I'm left to contemplate how two fixtures of Wall Street and global finance could take such clearly opposing views on Bitcoin, a sign in a shop window caught my eye. The sign — hanging in an absinthe shop — showed that they accept Bitcoin.

It happened to be the only shop I had seen in the Czech city over a four-day period where Bitcoin would be accepted. And I thought it quite curious that something not too recently outside the law in the United States, like absinthe, would be the kind of place to accept Bitcoin.

Figure 8-1: Bitcoin in Bohemia

But not everywhere is Bohemia, and not everyone in Bohemia will take Bitcoin. In fact, in Prague — even in 2018 — many vendors refuse to take credit cards.

There have been some big changes with Czech currency in recent years. While the Czech Republic is part of the European Union, it is not part of the European Monetary Union. This means it does not use the euro. In fact, it uses the Czech koruna. Now everything is denominated in koruna, but until the mid-to-late 2000s, other coins, called haléřů, which traded at 100 per koruna, were also in circulation. Prices have moved entirely away from using these lower-value coins made of aluminum.

I didn't know about the change, and I brought currency from my previous trips to Prague with me. This means that I had a bag of aluminum Czech pennies, which were valuable in 2002, somewhat less valuable in 2005, and which are now totally unspendable as prices have moved to whole koruny.

But despite this change in coin usage, you still need cash. Prague is a city now dominated by tourists, but you can't use credit cards everywhere. And you need cash often.

I wondered about the impossibility of needing cash and being unable to use Visa or my old haléřů. And yet there was a real prospect of using Bitcoin. Prague is clearly payments purgatory.

I wondered if paying for things in BTC in Bohemia would cause prices to rise in koruny — and if that might result in a further redenomination and future abandonment of certain koruna coins.

Or could it be that people excited about Bitcoin would find all the decimals confusing. Might Bitcoin users deem such fractional interests to be close to worthless, just based on the size of the average transaction?

The juice has to be worth the squeeze after all. And right now, that's barely justifiable. What would it be if a BTC were to hit a mythical figure like $100,000. Would you really be buying every $1 bottle of water with .00001 BTC?

Is that even a number people could conceptualize?

Maybe to a BTC owner this is good, because he or she won't care. It's a rounding error. But this could have two consequences:
1. The vendor could raise the BTC price of everyday items, which could spread inflation.
2. The vendor will continue to use the koruna that is practically easier to use from a computational standpoint.

Don't believe me? Consider these two examples:

After hyperinflation in Weimar Germany in the early 1920s, the German Rentenmark was exchanged for a new Reichsmark — at a rate of one trillion to one.[1]

More recently, in August 2018, Venezuela dropped five zeros from its currency, the bolivar, turning each 100,000 into just one.

These currencies were revalued to make computations easier and understandable.[2]

Looking Ahead

For now, Bitcoin is Bohemian even in Bohemia, where cash is still king. And the practicality of currency as a medium of exchange is unlikely to be replaced by transactions with lots of decimals.

This entire experience reminded me of a plane flight where I sat next to the head of sales for one of the biggest ATM installation companies in the world — a story I tell in more detail in my book *Jobs for Robots*. This executive told me that cash was absolutely critical for budgeting for lower-end-income individuals in a way that it would likely remain critical for certain parts of society for a very long time to come.

In the United States, you can go weeks without needing cash, but you can barely go a few hours in the Czech Republic. After all, each restroom requires you to pay, and none of them take anything other than cash. You can't use Bitcoin at the WC!

So, will Bitcoin leapfrog credit cards in a place that uses cash? Not likely. It's more likely to remain part of the kitsch-imbued ambiance of an absinthe shop for hipster tourists, rather than the face of a new future and emerging economic reality.

Furthermore, I also cannot imagine an absinthe bar having a dozen different logos for crypto on its door. One is enough to raise eyebrows. It seems unlikely that you would see a lot of different cryptos accepted everywhere. One or two are likely to win out, but which one is not yet assured. It might be Bitcoin.

But there are many big reasons why it might not be.

CHAPTER 9

DIE HARD CRYPTO

Maybe it is because the name Satoshi Nakamoto is fake and it sounds Japanese. Maybe it's because people use crypto for faceless, nameless, anonymous transactions that it evokes another fake Japanese-sounding name for me: Nakatomi Plaza.

This isn't a real place either. It's where the first *Die Hard* film takes place — where the villain of the movie, a thief-cum-terrorist Hans Gruber played by Alan Rickman is trying to steal bearer bonds.

And what are bearer bonds?

Well, that's the really interesting part: bearer bonds are a kind of bond that no longer exists. They are called bearer bonds because they are owned by the person who bears them.

If you have them in your possession, you own them. If you don't have them in your possession. You don't own them.

You can see a US bearer bond in Figure 9-1.

While bearer bonds were first issued in the United States in the second half of the nineteenth century, they stopped being issued in 1982.[1] Today, they are all but extinct. The reason? Anti-money laundering.

Anti-money laundering, or AML, as most finance people know it, is the set of legal initiatives taken by governments and financial institutions to prevent and hinder terrorists, criminals, and other bad actors from being able to engage in actions by making it difficult to transfer, hide, and otherwise use money.

Figure 9-1: US Government Bearer Bond[2]

And how was it that these bonds were so convenient for money laundering? Well, since these bonds were owned by the person who held them (i.e., the bearer), and there was no trading account or electronic or paper record required to redeem them, they could be bought, sold, and traded in an untraceable manner.

This means that bearer bonds can be used for money laundering and all kinds of other nefarious things. It's the reason the villain in the *Die Hard* movie wanted to get them, because they could not be traced, and they could be used for illegal activities.

Without any record keeping, bearer bonds could be easily used in illegal commerce without concern of detection because you wouldn't need to go into a Chase Bank branch or log into your Fidelity trading account to buy and sell them. You would, quite literally, take a suitcase of money and hand it to a fellow mobster or terrorist who would, in turn, give you the bearer bond.

So why do bearer bonds make me think of the interplay between Bitcoin and *Die Hard*?

That's simple.

Bitcoin and other cryptocurrencies can be used namelessly. Facelessly. Anonymously. They are digital bearer bonds.

And like physical bearer bonds before them, these digital bearer bonds are only owned by people who have the digital key. And they can be used for nefarious purposes.

But while bearer bonds are all but extinct because of AML initiatives, regulation has seriously lagged behind crypto. Bitcoin and cryptocurrencies are ascending, and they have not been outlawed in most countries despite their ease of use to violate AML laws.

The irony of cryptocurrencies, of course, is that the idea of non-government currency started as a vision of Austrian economists and free-market libertarians.

Yet while these same libertarians may praise the freedom of operating a currency outside of government, if their Bitcoin gets stolen, the police and the FBI will surely be their first phone call as a recourse of action. But it will be for naught. After all, even though transactions on the ledger are permanent, they cannot be tracked down because of the anonymity of cryptocurrencies.

So, as paragons of economic theory dream of the freedom crypto brings, the Hans Grubers of the world — including ISIS, anarchists, political subversives, organized criminals, and the rest of the digital underworld — rejoice in the ignorance and naïveté of those dreams.

CHAPTER 10

THE LAST BITCOIN

One thing Bitcoin fans rave about is the limited supply of bitcoin, which has only 21 million coins.[1] So far, 17 million have been mined.[2]

This amount has been laid out by Satoshi Nakamoto, and it underscores the importance of sound monetary policy. It stands in diametric opposition, from a theoretical standpoint, to the central bank policies of quantitative easing I discussed at length in Chapter 5.

The massive printing of currency and expanding central bank balance sheets present a risk of devaluation to the dollar, the euro, the Japanese yen, the British pound, and many other government-controlled fiat currencies.

And yet Bitcoin may be faced with a similar Faustian bargain.

You see, in this situation, the *Gretchenfrage* — the big question that will reveal all — is, Will we ever get to the last Bitcoin?[3]

Peak Bitcoin

Here's the thing about Bitcoin: as the number of Bitcoin reaches its inevitable end, miners may abandon the currency, and Bitcoin could similarly lose its marketability — and its value.

The price could rise for a time but then become worthless.

This is like the inevitable end of oil, a concept known as *Peak Oil*. Have you seen the old version of the movie *Mad Max* from 1979? A key theme of the movie and its franchise follow-ons is the hunt for the last gallon of gasoline in a post-apocalyptic world lacking natural resources — but having a violent road culture.

As someone who has spent 15 years covering oil markets, forecasting oil prices, and going to OPEC meetings, I know that we will never get to the last barrel of oil.

Never.

The reason: once the financial markets begin to price in actual peak oil supply, the demand will be driven by price to more fully embrace another form of transportation power. And we are nowhere near it yet. After all, liquid hydrocarbons are one of the most efficient and transportable forms of energy in history. And it's still relatively cheap. In the United States, the price of gasoline is about half the price in Europe.[4]

Now I know that some people reading this book may object and say that electric vehicles are an imminent inevitability. But I assure you, they are not imminent. Oil prices are still too low.

In fact, the outlook for electric vehicles is quite modest. Forecasts from the US Department of Energy show that only 12 percent of new car sales are likely to be electric by 2050.[5]

But eventually oil prices and gasoline prices will be much higher. And when they are, the mix of transportation energy sources will change. The market will adapt. But in a low-oil-price environment, the incentives are not there.

When the changes come, we won't need the last gallon of gasoline. We'll stop using it decades before we run out. And oil will be abandoned to the point that no one cares about the last barrel of oil, because oil will no longer serve any useful purpose.

And at some point, because its supply is limited, we may reach peak Bitcoin, too. At the 21 millionth bitcoin, no miner would have incentive to process the hash puzzles and the files that at the time could be multiple terabytes in size.

Miners will see they won't get any redemptions — they won't get any mining rewards from new Bitcoin — as the cap of 21 million approaches. This means that they may not mine the coins and transactions to 21 million at all. No reward means that there may be no mining. And so, just as with oil, we may never get to the last Bitcoin. Miners may just move on to other cryptocurrencies.

After the last Bitcoin is given out as a reward, there would be no way to buy or sell the Bitcoin. Its use as a medium of exchange would end along with its use as a store of value. After all, if something cannot be transferred, its value is only sentimental.

My mother saved her Beanie Babies to make very cute annual holiday displays, and I saved baseball cards from the late 1980s as a memento of collecting them with my father.

But I doubt any libertarians with an anarchist flare for the dystopian, who are hoping to buy a Lambo with their Bitcoin when the world economy and all fiat currencies cease to be useful, will be framing their Bitcoin encryption key for sentimental value and posterity on the mantle above their fireplace or in their children's hallway.

The Alternative

Peak Bitcoin could drive away Bitcoin users, investors, and miners. But Peak Bitcoin isn't the only potential path forward. There is still that Faustian deal I mentioned early in this chapter. And it's a doozy.

Peak Bitcoin could easily be avoided, because it isn't an inevitability. All that needs to happen is for Satoshi Nakamoto to increase the supply of Bitcoin.

It could still be used. It would keep the miners around.

And the logic behind the move would be that even though Bitcoin would be doing what every other currency issuer in the history of the world has ever done — devalued its currency and increased supply — it would be benevolent. It would be done right.

Yeah, right.

The guy who created Bitcoin is likely not named Satoshi Nakamoto. He isn't even likely one guy. And yet Satoshi should be — what? — trusted more than the central banks of long-established democratic governments?

I'm not buying it.

If Satoshi does take his digital bearer bonds corporate and increases the supply, thereby devaluing them, Bitcoin would be proven to be a currency that has a different means of transaction recordkeeping and a unique protocol of exchange. But it would no longer be a currency with a unique protocol for limiting supply and maintaining a store of value.

That's the Faustian deal Bitcoin may be forced to make:

Peak Bitcoin or *Sellout Bitcoin.*

Neither scenario would be likely good for its price, but at least in a sellout, people could dump their Bitcoin — or continue to use it as a useful medium of exchange. At Peak Bitcoin, however, HODLers (the people who plan to hold no matter what) could be stuck with something rare that no one wants.

Like Beanie Babies.

Or that last barrel of crude oil.

CHAPTER 11

TOO BIG TO SUCCEED

One of the biggest risks to Bitcoin and other blockchains is bloat. While a blockchain is a great way to keep track of every single transaction, it is not going to be small.

This is especially true of Bitcoin, which has now been around for almost a decade. The Bank of International Settlements (BIS) report from June 2018 noted that the Bitcoin blockchain was around 170 GB at that time — and that it was growing at a pace of 50 GB per year.[1]

The main impact of the expanding — bloating — size of the Bitcoin blockchain is that it slows down the transaction process and puts limits on the number of transactions that can be processed in a certain period of time.

The BIS is the central bank of central banks. And bloat was just one of the issues the BIS had with cryptocurrencies. The high energy demands of cryptocurrencies, the risk of fraud, and the ability to avoid direct regulation make the BIS a strong opponent.

I will discuss a number of these issues in Chapter 16, when we visit some of the main challenges facing cryptocurrencies — and some of the biggest threats to potential investors in the space.

As for the effectiveness of using a blockchain, or cryptocurrency, the number of transactions per second is a critical metric to evaluate. In Figure 11-1, I have shown the different transactions per second across a number of different payment processors. As you can see, the credit card company Visa absolutely crushes the competition at 24,000 transactions per second. Meanwhile Ripple, which I discuss in Chapter 7, is at a solid 1,500. Meanwhile, the beloved cryptocurrency Ethereum is at only 20. And Bitcoin is way down the line at only 7 transactions per second. That's very slow in comparison.

Figure 11-1: Transactions per Second[2]

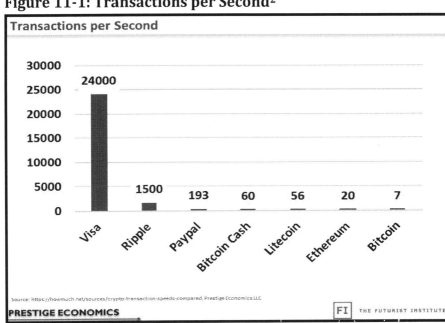

When we think about the potential tradeoffs of a blockchain, there is a clear tradeoff between speed and completeness. The reason it's important that all the transactions are right, is because there is no way to reverse the transactions in a blockchain.

This is very different than credit card companies that usually offer purchase protection for customer purchases. In other words, transactions can be unwound. And believe me, I am grateful for that kind of credit card protection.

When I bought my house back in 2013, I hired contractors to do work. They didn't complete it. And in the words of the home inspector who evaluated the house when I bought it and after the renovations, I was told that the home looked "more like it had been subject to vandalization than renovation." In his 40 years of experience, he said it was one of the 10 worst contractor jobs he had ever seen.

Fortunately, I paid for the contractor job with credit cards; my credit card company gave me a sizable amount back to compensate for the incomplete job and fire hazard repairs that were necessitated by the contractor's poor work.

Good thing I didn't pay for the job with Bitcoin! My money would have been gone. It would have been permanently on that ledger — a ways down from the Genesis Block. And there would have been no recourse to poor performance.

Most people who have returned defective items probably take for granted how easy it is to get a credit card refund from a store.

I've even had wire transfers accidentally go to the wrong account. One client transposed the routing number with the bank account number. With Ethereum or Litecoin? That money would have been permanently gone — inscribed onto the blockchain forever.

It's the same situation as with Bitcoin! It's permanent. It's done. The money is gone.

Good luck getting that cash back from the anonymized rando who just got paid, by the way!

In Chapter 8, I talked about the value of cash — and the potential difficulty in seeing a fully cashless society. Now, as we consider the potential to be cashless, it is also important to acknowledge the physical challenges and reality that cryptocurrencies in their current forms are not the best mediums of exchange that could supplant cash.

It's a simple matter of mechanics. The transactions cannot be processed quickly enough. I've often heard that everyone's biggest weakness is their greatest strength. And that their greatest strength is also their weakness. For Bitcoin, the public, permanent, and secure nature of the transactions is a plus that comes with a negative — bloat and a limited number of transactions per second.

This is why Bitcoin and other cryptocurrencies may be too big to succeed as mediums of exchange — even if they find uses as stores of value or digital bearer bonds as I noted in Chapter 9.

CHAPTER 12

FAKE NEWS AND CRYPTO

Journalism has become an unexpected part of my career. I gave my first interviews to print media and radio as an economist in 2004. This was followed shortly with television interviews across networks beginning in 2005 as well as some TV show guest hosting of Bloomberg television that has continued to the present. I even write the occasional column for Bloomberg.

My close relationship as a media source and on-air personality was part of the reason that I was invited to discuss the media's approach to the financial crisis at the event for the European Journalism Centre in late 2009, where I first heard the ideas of complimentary currency.

More recently, after building the coursework for The Futurist Institute, the Department of Defense flew me down to Tampa, Florida in December 2017 to speak about fake news. My presentation was titled "The Future of Fake News: Content Marketing, Click Funnels, and Counterterrorism." The attendees were senior-level government and military officials from NATO countries.

The event was the Joint Senior Psychological Operations Officers Conference. And the focus was on how the use of misinformation and disinformation on social media is used to manipulate the population on political issues.

My speech had three main points:

Content Marketing

Countless entities are generating content to drive traffic. Because so many different people and entities are creating this content, it is often difficult for people to tell what is good content and what is garbage. Gone are the days when everyone knew that the magazines at supermarket checkout counters about aliens meeting with the president and the infamous Bat Boy are fake.

Clickfunnels

Companies push potential customers through a funnel to become loyal followers and promoters of their brand. But they do not care how many people they lose during a marketing campaign to get those loyal followers and promoters. They only care about getting *some*. Terrorists and subversives also use this strategy.

Cryptocurrency

Terrorists, anarchists, and politically subversive entities can use social media to boost their profile and disseminate their messaging. And they can fund their activities with untraceable cryptocurrencies. Gone are the days when spies and terrorists needed to smuggle diamonds, bars of gold, or suitcases of cash. Now they can easily launder money using cryptocurrencies, which I discuss in Chapter 16 and show in Figure 16-1.

Facebook Kept All the Money

At the time I gave my talk in early December 2017, it was clear that Facebook and other social media had been used as part of Russian PsyOps — psychological operations — during the 2016 US presidential election.

And it was clear that they were keeping the cash.

If any media company in the world outside of social media had been the victim of foreign PsyOps, they would not have kept the money. *The New York Times*, *Bloomberg*, *Fox Business*, *MSNBC*, and even regional papers would not have kept the money — or at least not all of it. They would have probably issued an apology, and then they almost certainly would have donated the money to (or created) a charity.

But not Facebook.

Facebook kept the money.

In my talk, I stressed the need for regulation, oversight, and a crackdown on cryptocurrencies. And I was not alone in addressing this national security risk. Awareness of these issues was just beginning to percolate to the powers that be at the time, but it was clear that big changes were coming. I cautioned our clients in late 2017, after my speech in Tampa, about the coming potential regulation and an imminent crackdown on cryptocurrencies. At the time, Bitcoin and many crypto prices were near their all-time highs. But it was becoming clear how bad actors were using cryptocurrencies for nefarious purposes.

Since my talk in Tampa, major global entities have issued similar warnings about cryptocurrencies and their extralegal nature. Christine Lagarde, the head of the International Monetary Fund, noted at a conference titled *Terrorism financing: the other war against Al-Qaida and Daesh,* on 26 April 2018, that

> There are still challenges to the effectiveness of counter-terrorism financing efforts. These include improving our understanding of terrorism financing risks, making better use of financial intelligence, and enhancing domestic and international cooperation. Fintech was another area explored during the conference. **It can be used to promote and fund terrorism through the anonymity of crypto-assets.** But leveraged effectively, fintech can also be a powerful tool to fight terrorism and its financing.[1]

The Bank of International Settlements, which is considered the central bank of central banks, noted in June 2018 that

> They lack a legal entity or person that can be brought into the regulatory perimeter. **Cryptocurrencies live in their own digital, nationless realm and can largely function in isolation from existing institutional environments or other infrastructure.** Their legal domicile — to the extent they have one — might be offshore, or impossible to establish. As a result, they can be regulated only indirectly.[2]

The big takeaway is that cryptocurrencies exist outside of legal frameworks and their anonymity facilitates terrorism funding.

CHAPTER 13

BEYOND CRYPTO: CORPORATE VALUE OF THE BLOCKCHAIN

The potential impact of blockchain is bigger than most people can imagine but not nearly as great as some believe. And while many people think blockchain is just crypto, that's only the tip of the iceberg. This was the cornerstone of a talk I gave at SXSW in March 2017.

The impact on corporate supply chains — on logistics, transport, and freight — is going to be massive. And there are a number of other industries, like finance and agriculture, where a chain of custody of ownership and good record keeping is likely to provide a significant value proposition for blockchain.

After all, blockchain allows for a permanent distributed ledger, and if used in a private, commercial endeavor, it could provide instant transparency of origin, content, and custody, which is often required from a regulatory framework for conflict minerals, chemical content, or trade. And this kind of transparency can all have significant value from a public health and safety standpoint, as is the case with agricultural products and food safety.

The potential for blockchain to add economic value in many different industries and corporate fields is massive. But it isn't equal across industries. The biggest value proposition is where there are supply chains and risks to mitigate, as well as health and safety issues.

Assets in Transition See Greatest Use Case

The value proposition for using blockchains for record keeping on long-lived assets is lower than for assets that move. This is true whether we are talking about financial assets that frequently move between investments, markets, and parties — or assets that physically move or are in flux. This impacts The Futurist Institute's assessment for blockchain use potential in Figure 13-1.

Figure 13-1: Assessment of Blockchain Potential

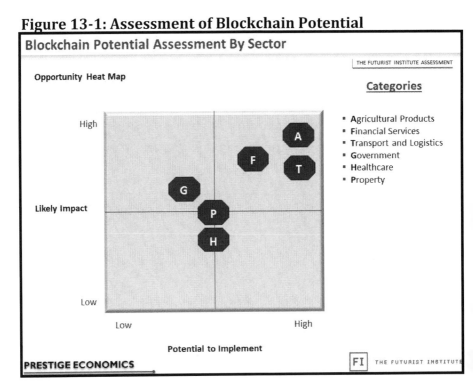

In addition to movement factors driving the use case and value proposition for blockchain, there are limitations on blockchain's potential uses in some industries, as I will discuss in Chapter 14, due to incumbent regulatory requirements and legal frameworks — especially in the United States. This is why healthcare, property, and government data uses for blockchain may prove more limited than for agricultural products, transport and logistics, and financial services.

Commercial Structure of Blockchains

As I discussed in Chapter 4, blockchains can be customized. In a practical implementation sense, the major choices to be made are shown in Figure 13-2. This includes choices about who can access a blockchain as well as who can write transactions and use it.

Figure 13-2: Commercial Blockchain Potential[1]

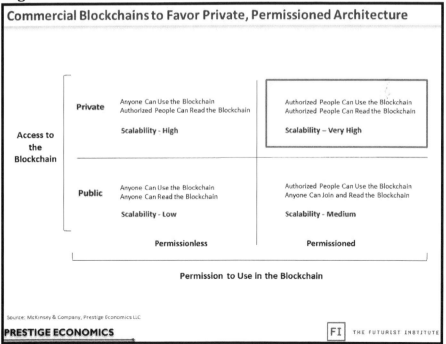

Commercial Blockchains to Favor Private, Permissioned Architecture

		Permissionless	Permissioned
Access to the Blockchain	Private	Anyone Can Use the Blockchain Authorized People Can Read the Blockchain Scalability - High	Authorized People Can Use the Blockchain Authorized People Can Read the Blockchain Scalability – Very High
	Public	Anyone Can Use the Blockchain Anyone Can Read the Blockchain Scalability - Low	Authorized People Can Use the Blockchain Anyone Can Join and Read the Blockchain Scalability - Medium

Permission to Use in the Blockchain

Source: McKinsey & Company, Prestige Economics LLC

PRESTIGE ECONOMICS

FI   THE FUTURIST INSTITUTE

This illustration is based on a framework presented in a McKinsey report on blockchain. The report thesis — and an argument I agree with — is that the commercial use cases for blockchains are likely to foster a commercial preference for private blockchains that require special permissions.

I have often referenced blockchain as a database technology with specialized permissions. This means that while there may be a permanent, distributed record of transactions, not everyone will be able to see or access those transactions, and specialized permission will be required to use the blockchain. The McKinsey report identifies this type of blockchain as very scalable. I agree.

The ability to scale up the use of a database is easiest when there are limitations on who can use it. And there are critical tradeoffs with blockchain. The computational power, cost, and energy required will be determined by the complexity of the cryptography, the volume of transactions, and the desired speed.

And a private blockchain with limitations of use is likely to require much less electricity, computer processing power, and time than a public, permissionless blockchain like Bitcoin.

Blockchain Disruption in Finance

One of the topics of my book *Jobs for Robots*, is the notion of FinTech disruption potential for financial services. This remains a critical concern when it comes to blockchain. As in other areas of high value propositions for blockchain use, most of financial services is transactions based — and not tied to long-lived assets.

After all, financial assets — like stocks — are usually traded and exchanged with much greater frequency than a house or piece of land. And there are regulatory mandates to track financial transactions, due to their liquidity, potential misuse, and the transparent value of those assets.

This is why there are significant value propositions and use cases for blockchain in the field of finance.

Autonomous Research and Procensus conducted a survey on expectations about the top areas in which investors and investment professionals expect disruption from blockchain. Clearing & settlement was expected to be the most likely field of finance to first be disrupted by blockchain according to 43 percent of investors and 39 percent of industry professionals who were surveyed.[2] The other three categories included cross-border payments, mobile payments, and trust & custody. The responses reflect how important the expected disruption from blockchain is for financial services fields — especially for moving and tracking funds.

In my opinion, this result is likely due to the fact that more transparent data in a blockchain would likely allow for a more rapid or easier clearing and settlement process, which can sometimes hold up funds and delay payments. In other words, using a blockchain could accelerate the ability to move funds. Plus, the payments categories are also about moving funds. And while trust & custody is focused on ownership, it also impacts the ability to move funds. In short, this survey reflects blockchain's expected disruption for moving funds and financial records.

The Futurist Institute's Financial Services Assessment

As the Chairman of The Futurist Institute, I directed an analysis and study of corporate and commercial opportunities in blockchain across industries. The overview is in Figure 13-1.

In Figure 13-3, I show The Futurist Institute's assessment of the potential uses of blockchain in financial services. The areas where we see the most potential and greatest likelihood for blockchain use overall are in the areas of trade finance and B2B payments. This reflects a focus on corporate transactions as being of both the highest value and greatest importance from financial record keeping and commercial standpoints. In other words, using blockchains in these areas is likely to bring significant value to large entities — and the economy overall.

Figure 13-3: Financial Services Blockchain Assessment

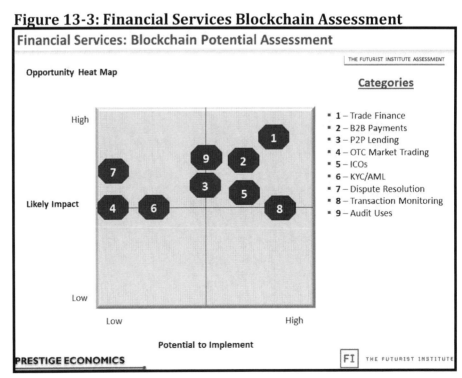

From an oversight and regulatory standpoint, we see a high potential for blockchain implementation in transaction monitoring. This is not, however, something I would identify as a high-value activity for the economy. After all, it is a layer of oversight and regulation, but not necessarily something that would likely contribute to the operational ROI of a business. The potential to reduce fraud, however, could generate value.

Areas with a low potential in financial services, in our estimation, are in more complicated financial markets like over-the-counter (OTC) trading. In many cases, annotating and tracking complicated financial structures could prove cumbersome. After all, financial exchanges are very sophisticated, and if these OTC transactions are too complicated for exchanges, it seems likely that they may require a lot of handcranking, in which case a blockchain may not prove useful. And since these are relatively rare, it may not be very impactful for the financial services industry or the economy overall.

Blockchain is likely to be used in a number of other areas as well. But one topic that might stand out in Figure 13-3 is our assessment of the use of blockchain for ICOs. Although blockchain has been inherently tied to cryptocurrencies as the technology that powers them, the regulatory risks for initial coin offerings present a potential limit on financial benefits.

Often described as a pre-revenue IPO, ICOs could come under more regulatory oversight, hampering or killing them — and the use of blockchain in their execution.

The Futurist Institute's Transport and Logistics Assessment

Finance gets a lot of attention when it comes to blockchain use and potential. But transport, logistics, and freight are, in our estimation, the areas with the highest potential for blockchain adoption — and sources of the highest potential accretive value creation for commercial interests and the economy.

There are two big areas where we see blockchain use cases for transport and logistics: increasing the ease of physical transport and exchange of goods as well as regulatory compliance. Both of these depend on keeping a clean chain of custody and having easy-to-demonstrate records about the content and origination of goods.

Figure 13-4: Transport and Logistics Blockchain Assessment

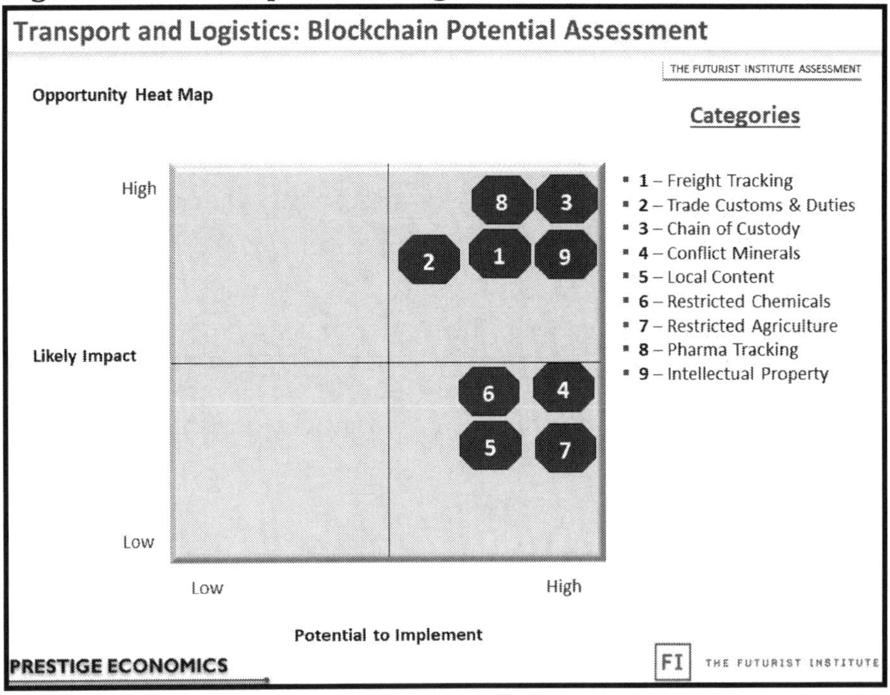

Transport and Logistics: Blockchain Potential Assessment

THE FUTURIST INSTITUTE ASSESSMENT

Opportunity Heat Map

Categories

* **1** – Freight Tracking
* **2** – Trade Customs & Duties
* **3** – Chain of Custody
* **4** – Conflict Minerals
* **5** – Local Content
* **6** – Restricted Chemicals
* **7** – Restricted Agriculture
* **8** – Pharma Tracking
* **9** – Intellectual Property

High

8 3

2 1 9

Likely Impact

6 4

5 7

Low

Low   High

Potential to Implement

PRESTIGE ECONOMICS

FI THE FUTURIST INSTITUTE

Transport, logistics, and freight are industries with a high degree of what economists call *transactional friction*. This means that there is a great deal of paperwork and expenses required to facilitate trade and physical movement and exchange of goods. This is an ideal use case for blockchain, which provides a distributed record that be can be set within a predefined network to ease and reduce that transactional friction. Basically, it would make the transport and exchange of goods faster and cheaper.

Like finance, transactions in transport, logistics, and freight are frequent. This stands in stark contrast to the transfer of physical properties. And it ties back to our contention that the greatest potential use case and source of value for blockchain will be in industries where there is a high number of transactions.

Furthermore, like finance, some aspects of freight and transport are regulated. This is especially true for some manufacturing restrictions of use for some chemicals and conflict metals. Plus, counterfeiting is a significant problem for some high-value goods in the supply chain, like pharmaceuticals, certain manufactured goods like inverted delta parts, and military weaponry. And there's also high tech goods, like smartphones. Blockchain use could increase transparency in these supply chains, reducing potential fraud, increasing safety, and saving companies money.

The Futurist Institute's Agriculture Assessment
One of the greatest industries with the potential for blockchain use is in the field of agriculture. As in the areas of finance and transport, the use cases and value proposition in agriculture are tied to transaction frequency.

Of course, blockchain isn't going to help you milk cows or grow corn faster. But it is likely to be important for tracking the origin of foodstuffs by knowing its custody and by having a transparent supply chain that facilitates trade and transactions.

The high public value — and economic value — of blockchains in agriculture is highly documented. Every time there is some kind of food contamination, it becomes a national crisis, because the exact origins of affected products are not known.

In my opinion, this is ridiculous. If I can track every bottle of shampoo or bag of dog treats that I order online, how are we not already tracking where every bag of salad, box of cereal, and egg comes from? Seriously. Why are we not already doing this?

Figure 13-5: Agriculture Blockchain Assessment

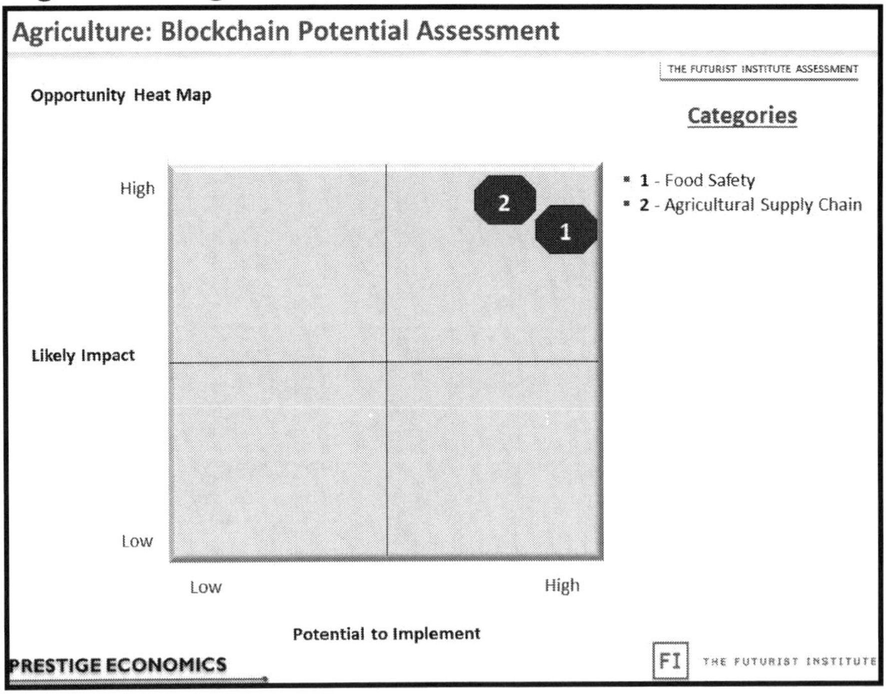

Agriculture: Blockchain Potential Assessment

Opportunity Heat Map

THE FUTURIST INSTITUTE ASSESSMENT

Categories

1 - Food Safety
2 - Agricultural Supply Chain

Likely Impact — High / Low

Potential to Implement — Low / High

PRESTIGE ECONOMICS

FI THE FUTURIST INSTITUTE

The lacking transparency about the origins of foodstuffs is shockingly absent. And should already be in place. But even if we discount this abject negligence of tracking that has public health implications, there is also a massive financial value proposition from tracking food. After all, every time there is a food contamination issue with E.coli, millions of dollars of food is simply disposed of.

This is a waste on so many levels. And blockchain can help to ameliorate both the food safety risks and the risks of financial loss. This is reflected in The Futurist Institute's expectations for agriculture and blockchain in Figure 13-5.

One Caveat About Risk

There is one caveat I would offer about the corporate use of blockchain. It is not a 100% guarantee about the products involved. There is still a need for people involved in the network to behave honestly and ethically. If someone in the system is a bad actor, there will still be adverse economic consequences. And if we trust in blockchain absolutely, the consequences could be even greater than in our current system.

This does not mean blockchain should not be used. It should, because it has value, it can improve recordkeeping, reduce transactional frequency, and contribute positively to public health.

But we need to remember the human elements of risk that exist in every system. I discuss this further in Chapter 16.

CHAPTER 14

PRACTICAL LIMITATIONS FOR INDUSTRY BLOCKCHAINS

In some ways, blockchain is a technology that seems custom made for industries with high transaction volume and tracking regulatory and safety requirements, like finance, transport and logistics, and agriculture. But these are not the only industries for which blockchain is likely to have some high-value use cases — even if they are likely to be the most straightforward.

Other industries to which blockchain can add value are likely to face adoption challenges due to low transaction volume or incumbent regulatory requirements and legal frameworks. In the United States, this includes the industries of property (or real estate), government, and healthcare.

Building blockchain networks for these industries, often typified by legal constraints and regulations, presents some major issues. The greatest of these is the potential for permanent, unwindable transactions.

The Futurist Institute's Property Assessment

Maybe you've heard that property is nine-tenths of the law. For blockchain, tracking these transactions presents outsized value, compared to many other industries. And this is why the transfer of property could be a challenge for blockchain. After all, the legal permanence of blockchain transactions is a great plus for logistics and finance chain of custody, but it could prove to be a nightmare in the transfer of physical property. After all, how could a court unwind a permanently recorded transaction?

The first step for a blockchain's value in property would be to become a digital and permanent Domesday Book, in which land is registered. Until all property is registered electronically, it would be impossible to engage in transactions of property.

Figure 14-1: Property Blockchain Assessment

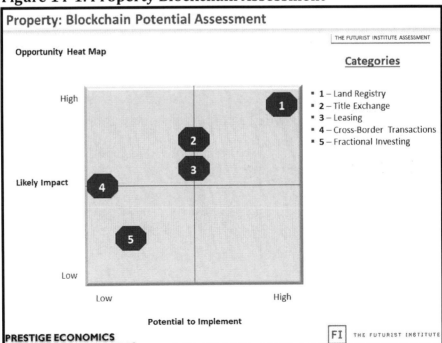

But blockchain use elsewhere in real property is likely to be slow going. And it's the same reason why the real estate industry seems antiquated at times: the inefficient and disjointed system of records of property. Only with the consolidation of records could title be assured. And this could take a very, very long time.

Blockchain experts love to talk about the potential to transfer property easily with a digital blockchain. But there are major risks associated with this concept. After all, there are risks that the historical title of a property may not be clean. This can result in legal issues, and it is why many people buy title insurance.

With a blockchain, the transfer of ownership would exist as a permanent record on the ledger. This means that amending the transaction would not be as simple as adding an amendment or codicil or other agreement to the paper or digital records. After all, the blockchain is permanent. This means that while the future transfer of real property could be made much easier with a blockchain, it could get more sticky in transactions where there are problems.

To add a comparative context, trading shares of stock or making international payments or shipments seems ideal for blockchain. But real estate and real property transactions are usually complicated, valuable, and infrequent enough to warrant people in the process for some time to come. This is especially true for very complicated cross-border transactions and for fractional investing. In these areas, blockchain seems much less likely to be used, due to their potentially high complexity.

As for leases, this is an area where blockchain seems wholly unnecessary. Remember that a blockchain is not easy to construct or transact on, and that there can also be energy and computational costs. Using DocuSign and other forms of electronic signature agreements is likely to be fine for leases for a long time to come.

The Futurist Institute's Government Assessment
Another area that's a mixed bag for its future blockchain prospects is government. Some areas, like government procurement, government spending, and tax records, are ideally suited for blockchain use. But other areas, like voting and identity registration, are not, in part due to potential Constitutional constraints.

Figure 14-2: Government Blockchain Assessment

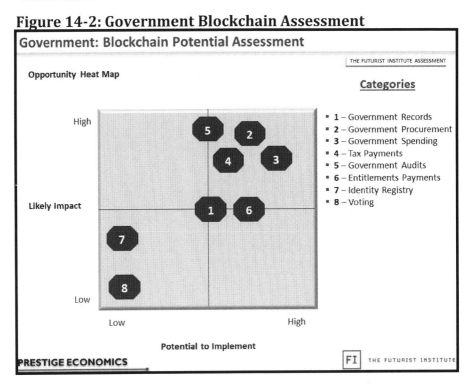

As with finance, logistics, and agriculture, the reason for blockchain's significant use cases and value propositions in government is tied to frequency of transactions. The transaction volume and need to track money coming in and going out presents the potential for blockchain use. This is especially true in the case of government spending and procurement, because of the need for transparency.

It may be that some of these government blockchains fall under the framework of a public blockchain with permissioned use, as shown in Figure 13-2. This is the case where anyone can see or join the blockchain, but only permissioned parties may transact using it. But the public nature of the blockchain would not be without tradeoffs, and it would elevate the need for cybersecurity and cryptographic complexity. It could also slow the potential transaction rate and increase the energy and computational requirements to process the blocks on publicly visible chains.

The use of blockchains could add value for government (so-called "Yellow Book") audits, which operate under Generally Accepted Government Auditing Standards, which are set out by the US Government Accountability Office.[1] Fraud and other major concerns in government audits could be reduced with greater transparency from blockchain use. Of course, before these blockchains can be used for audits, they need to be used for transactional purposes that would be the subject of the government entities under audit. In other words, there would first need to be blockchains for tracking government procurement and spending, as well as the collection of taxes and the issuing of entitlements payments.

The final area of government blockchain that has been considered is for voting and identity registration. This is likely to be used in some countries. After all, electronic voting by cellphone already exists in some countries like Estonia, which instituted it in 2011.[2] But I wouldn't expect this in the United States anytime soon.

There are currently ongoing debates in the United States about voter registration identification. The use of blockchain for voting seems unlikely. Furthermore, given the current political climate, the use of a blockchain to register citizens, legal residents, and individuals who may not legally be in the country would be a massive political hot potato.

So don't expect to see a blockchain registry of every person anytime soon. And the truth is that it may not be needed, as the US government already has people's Social Security numbers. There may not be a national registry of property ownership, for which records are disjointed and often maintained at the state, county, or local level, but the US government does have Social Security numbers for individuals.

And while the Social Security system is incomplete and the use of paper cards with these nine-digit numbers on them seems at times laughable, it may be preferable to an unnecessary political hot potato that could cause legal issues, a potential Constitutional crisis, and even societal unrest. Plus, the potential for Kafkaesque problems that could occur with a permanent population ledger is limitless. What if you are accidentally declared deceased? The blockchain would be permanent after all.

The Futurist Institute's Government Assessment

The field of healthcare is one of the most mixed industries with blockchain use cases and value propositions. On the one hand, you have records that have only recently been transitioned from paper to electronic form — and you still have many healthcare documents that are maintained in paper form.

So, the need for records to be maintained permanently and be easily transferred is clear. This is especially important to maintain proper patient care. But on the other hand, you have a need for patient privacy. This means that the data that could be transferred on a blockchain would need to have significant cryptographic security elements, which would make it slow to use and would require more computer power and electricity.

Figure 14-3: Healthcare Blockchain Assessment

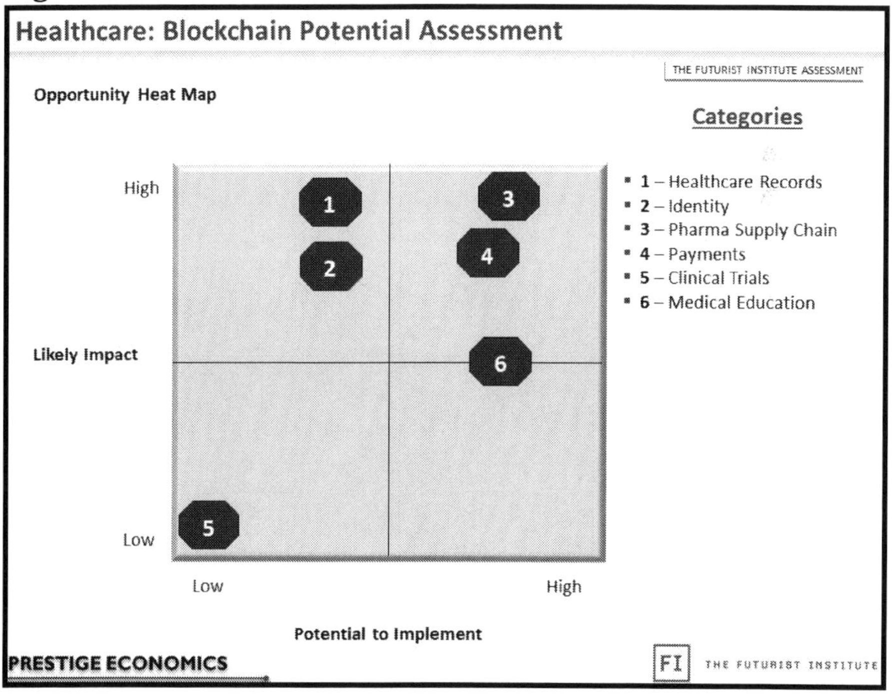

Healthcare: Blockchain Potential Assessment
THE FUTURIST INSTITUTE ASSESSMENT
Opportunity Heat Map
Categories
1 – Healthcare Records
2 – Identity
3 – Pharma Supply Chain
4 – Payments
5 – Clinical Trials
6 – Medical Education
High
Likely Impact
Low
1
2
3
4
5
6
Low
High
Potential to Implement
PRESTIGE ECONOMICS
FI
THE FUTURIST INSTITUTE

These factors could hinder healthcare blockchain adoption for individual identity and healthcare records. But there are some important use cases for blockchain in healthcare.

As in the other fields, blockchain has the greatest potential and use case with frequent transactions, which is why we see the potential for blockchain use with healthcare payments. And we all see the need for pharmaceutical supply chains to be secure, which has both public health and intellectual property value propositions. After all, you don't want to get the wrong medicine. And a company doesn't want you getting counterfeit drugs that undercut their profitability.

The final two areas of healthcare that we have considered at The Futurist Institute are clinical trials and medical education. For clinical trials we see blockchain as completely unnecessary, as most of these trials are done in a handful of places with a handful of people, and they are often run from one central location. The distributed nature of the blockchain would not be useful in such cases. As for medical education, blockchain could be helpful for recordkeeping, but this is more a compliance issue than an economically accretive activity. It is unlikely to be a high value-add use of a blockchain.

A Mix of Industries and Activities

Some industries are a natural fit for blockchain use. But other industries are not. While property, government, and healthcare are not natural fits for the technology, some of the high-volume transactional, financial, and large-scope record keeping could prove valuable use cases for blockchain.

CHAPTER 15

INVESTING IN BLOCKCHAIN AND CRYPTO

Let me start off by sharing the first rule of investing: **Do not invest in things you do not understand.**

Other financial professionals may take umbrage at that statement, noting that diversity is rule number one, but I don't care. **Do not put your money in something that does not make sense.**

That being said, a lot of ICOs, many blockchain investments, and a number of cryptocurrencies do not make sense. In 2017 and early 2018, Bitcoin prices skyrocketed! And the prospects of getting very rich quickly fueled the greatest financial bubble in the history of the world in late 2017 and early 2018.

This has led to one of the strangest experiences of my 15-year career in finance. In Chapter 17, I relate some of my favorite stories about the uniqueness of the investing landscape against a backdrop of a fairly normal historical context that blockchain fills as a database used for transactional permanence.

The Hype Correlation

In December 2017, as the price of Bitcoin surged, I saw a sign on the side of the road near my house that said "Bitcoin ATM." It was next to a sign for "We buy houses." As the kids say, "seems legit." But only ironically.

In fact, the number of scams around Bitcoin and ICOs became a massive problem. In April 2018, the Texas State Securities Board published a scathing report about scams.[1]

The price surge in Bitcoin pulled in massive interest around ICOs and blockchain. The volume surged on price, as you can see in Figure 15-1, but so did the question on Google, "What is Bitcoin?" You can see the spike in Google searches in Figure 15-2.

Figure 15-1: The Price of Bitcoin[2]

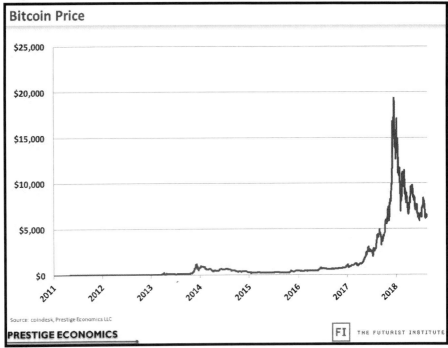

Source: coindesk, Prestige Economics LLC

PRESTIGE ECONOMICS

FI | THE FUTURIST INSTITUTE

Figure 15-2: Google Trends "What is Bitcoin?"[3]

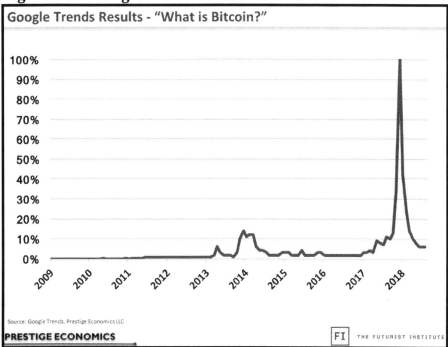

Figure 15-3: Daily Bitcoin Transaction Volume[4]

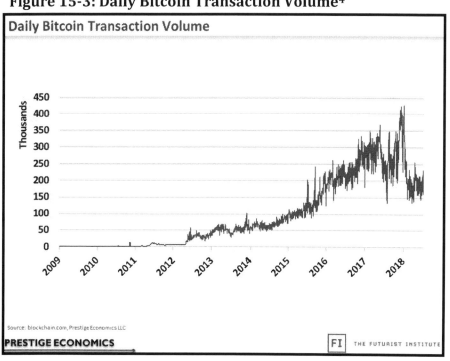

These Google searches indicate the attraction to Bitcoin as an investment by people who did not even know the first thing about it. And dumb money followed lucky money.

One person I know wrote on LinkedIn, "I'm mad about Bitcoin. Because I don't get it. And I didn't get any."

At least he didn't invest in something he did not understand. But many did. And the rise in transaction volumes seen in Figure 15-3 shows a very close relationship between the transaction volume and the price of Bitcoin. Of course, the Google search "What is Bitcoin?" has also been highly correlated with the price of Bitcoin.

Beyond Bitcoin

Some of the investments in altcoins and ICOs were knock-on effects of a surging price in Bitcoin. You can see the correlations between ICO and Bitcoin ROI through March 2018, as well as Bitcoin and ICO monthly returns in percentage terms.

Some investors were true believers in the companies offering tokens and coins, but most were trying to get rich quick. And let's not forget the FOMO crowd.

In recent years there has been a growing contingent of investors who could be classified as having FOMO — or a fear of missing out — on the next tech revolution. Maybe they have regrets for not investing Apple or Amazon when it was cheap, and the behavioral investing phenomenon of regret pulled them into the mix, with hopes of finding the next Apple or Amazon — or at least outsized financial returns and Lambos, as noted in Chapter 7.

Figure 15-4: Average Amount Raised by ICOs[5]

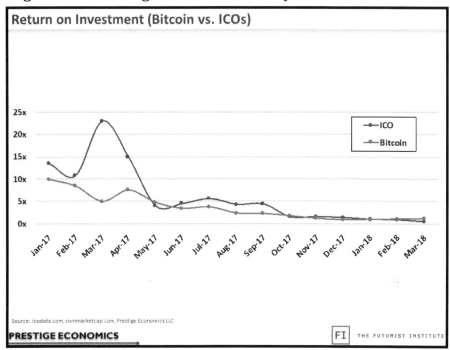

Figure 15-5: Total Funds Raised by ICOs[6]

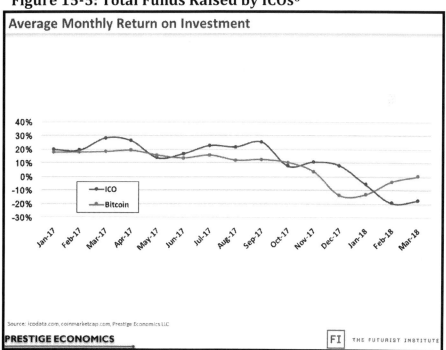

Does Your Dog Need a Podcast?

In 2017, I wrote an article titled, "Does Your Dog Need a Podcast?"[7] Although this article praised podcasts as a means to build an online audience and share valuable content, it was actually inspired by my experience as an angel investor. I was faced with a prospective deal in early 2017 to fund a podcast with a high valuation, high expenses, no revenue, and a very, very small listener base.

Shockingly, the podcast got funded.

Tech fever spread to ICOs, which enjoyed massively positive ROIs in 2017 through March 2018 (Figure 15-6) and monthly positive double-digit returns almost every month in 2017 (Figure 15-7). But ICOs came under increased scrutiny and regulation in 2018, in order — in part — to protect naïve investors. Subsequently, monthly ICO returns have generally fallen in 2018.

To give you an idea of what some of these ICO coins and tokens are like, I would share that some of them have names that cannot even be spoken in polite company. And they are worth millions.

While some ICOs and some cryptocurrencies may survive the increased scrutiny, skepticism, and proper regulation, most of them are unlikely to make it. As for those that survive, if they are utility tokens, you would not actually own a stake in that company as you would with an IPO. The utility tokens would just give you the ability to use the company's service in the future. They are, as I have described in Chapter 7, like Disney Dollars or Groupons.

Figure 15-6: Average Amount Raised by ICOs[8]

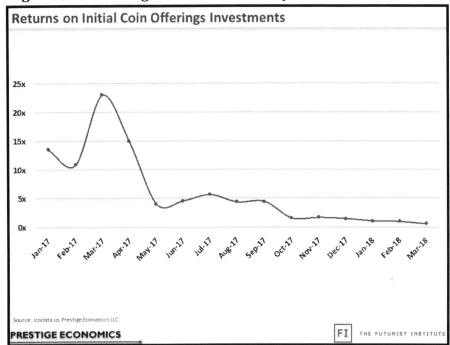

Figure 15-7: Total Funds Raised by ICOs[9]

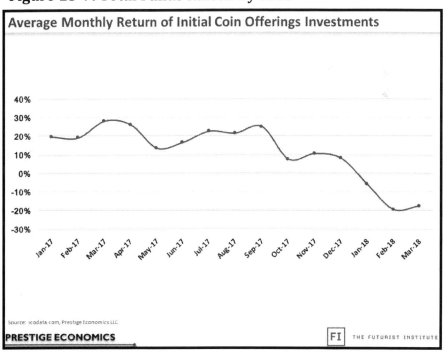

Investing in Blockchain

Along with the direct investments in ICOs and cryptocurrencies, there has also been massive investment in blockchain. Unlike ICOs and cryptocurrencies, which face significant regulatory risks, blockchain has tremendous promise and offers a massive value proposition in commercial and corporate use cases, which was the subject of Chapters 13 and 14.

As blockchain needs rise, this will create significant professional and business opportunities — for developers, consultants, and strategists. But even as blockchain presents opportunities, it is best to remember not to invest in things you do not understand.

And for those companies looking to pull a fast one and rebrand as a blockchain entity, the regulators are watching them, too.

In December 2017, near the height of the Bitcoin price bubble, an iced tea company, Long Island Iced Tea Corp., announced a name change to Long Blockchain Corp. This name change caused the company's price to spike from around $2 per share to almost $7 per share. An investigation into the company was subsequently launched, and the price of the company came crashing down to around $0.34 per share as of 1 August 2018.[10]

The NASDAQ also delisted the company, removing it from its public equity exchange, and the US Securities and Exchange Commission subpoenaed the organization on 10 July 2018. This does not seem to bode well for its management, and it should serve as a cautionary tale about trying to ride a bubble, the power of regulators, and the hype around blockchain.

CHAPTER 16

TRUSTLESS TRUST AND DIGITAL CURRENCY RISKS

When people talk about digital currencies and blockchain technology, they are often quick to reference "trustless trust." Although this is a mantra in the world of blockchain, it goes too far.

Even Satoshi referenced "cryptographic proof instead of trust."[1]

Because that's all a blockchain can ensure, cryptographic proof. It cannot provide trust, and it cannot guarantee that people participating in a blockchain will be honest.

As my wife says, "Trust no randos!"

But that's exactly what you do in an anonymous cryptocurrency blockchain like the one that powers Bitcoin.

Personally, I would much rather have the protection afforded by Visa and financial institutions than an anonymous blockchain for all of my transactions. That does not mean that cryptocurrencies and blockchains are not valuable. But they do come with risks — for individuals and corporations.

Fraud and ICOs

As we've covered in the previous chapter, there are pretty big risks in making investments in things you don't understand.

With ICOs, there are very big regulatory risks, where you may buy utility tokens for companies that never actually produce anything you can use them for.

In fact, the Bank of International Settlements, which published a report about cryptocurrencies that I discussed in Chapter 11, noted that cryptocurrency prices react strongly to shutdowns of illegal marketplaces and that a large share of initial coin offerings are thought to be fraudulent.[2]

And then there's the real illegal stuff.

Money of The Criminal Underworld

Cryptocurrencies aren't just a part of the gimmick economy that has been fueled by a raging case of tech fever. They are also part of the global black market. I've discussed this to a certain degree in Chapter 12, where criminal, terrorist, and politically subversive elements have used cryptocurrencies to fund activities below the radar of law enforcement.

The actual way that money laundering can occur with cryptocurrencies is laid out in Figure 16-1. This is one of the biggest value propositions of cryptocurrencies and an anonymous payment system with unbreakable cryptography.

And when you lie down with dogs, you often wake with fleas.

Figure 16-1: Money Laundering with Crypto[3]

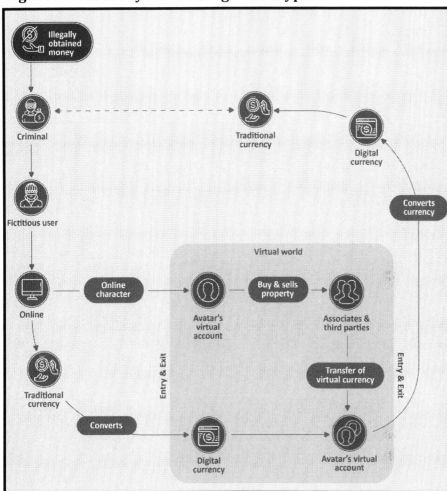

Figure 16-2: Cryptocurrency Theft in 2017[4]

This is why cryptocurrency is often a means of theft and other illegal activities. Since you already have bad actors engaging in criminal activity by laundering their funds, it should not be a surprise that they may try to hack your wallet, hit you with a Ponzi scheme, engage in phishing, or make you subject to ransomware. The graphic in Figure 16-2 shows just some of the illegal activities that hit the cryptocurrency space in 2017. The costs were staggering.

According to a Bloomberg article from 27 June 2018, the FBI had 130 ongoing cryptocurrency related investigations on its books. [5]

Even in my own LinkedIn feed in 2018, I experienced one of these attacks. This was a two-pronged scam, and I am sure it works sometimes. First, they tried to hit my network with a scam. And then they tried to guilt me into sending crypto.

It started when someone spoofed me — they created a profile just like mine, with the same picture, historical work experience, and name. Then they commented within the body of a post I had made and offered three free Ethereum to anyone who would send one Ethereum, so that their account could be confirmed.

It was a ridiculous offer. But they don't need too many people to fall for that kind of Ponzi scheme to make money. I quickly deleted the fake post requesting ETH, and I reported it. The profile was quickly disabled. But then I began to receive messages from a guy who claimed he had sent the one Ethereum. He wanted to know where his 3 Ethereum were. Naturally, I blocked him as well.

Chances are, it was the same entity asking where his Ethereum was as the entity asking other people to send one Ethereum, you know, just to confirm their super-secret, anonymous cryptocurrency address. The scammers likely figure that if they can't trick people into a Ponzi scheme, maybe they can guilt me into thinking someone fell into it because of me. And it's all untraceable.

Cybersecurity Risks and Blockchain

There are also risks from using a blockchain that go beyond cryptocurrency scams. And it's called the attack surface.

I recently completed a certificate in cybersecurity with Carnegie Mellon University's Software Engineering Institute in conjunction with the National Association of Corporate Directors, of which I am a Governance Fellow. At the end, I had three big takeaways that are relevant for blockchain.

The first notion is the concept of **resilience**. This means, can your company bounce back? It is a question intrinsically linked at the hip a bit with the notion of survivability. In other words, will your company survive a cyberattack, or will it cease to be a going concern? When I think of resilience, I think of blockchain's value in reducing the central point of failure risks that I discussed in Chapter 3.

The second concept that was put forward in the course was the notion of **resource management**. This is the idea that you cannot do everything you want with the security of a company. And the same, of course, is true with the use of blockchains.

I have often referenced the massive computer-processing and energy-power requirements for Bitcoin transactions. The same is true with considering the use of a blockchain for commercial and corporate purposes in terms of time, processing power, and electricity. Sometimes the juice may not be worth the squeeze, and blockchain is not for everything.

The third cybersecurity concept, and the most important for blockchain to consider, is **attack surface**. The attack surface of an entity is the amount of different points and places that an entity is exposed and at risk of a cyberattack or cyber threat. The attack surface may actually be larger, and the risk bigger, for a company using a blockchain.

When we consider the fact that a corporate or commercial blockchain is likely to be distributed among many parties, you realize that the attack surface may be much larger than a company that uses a database with a small finance team of just a few people sitting in an office in a centralized location.

If you work in a company where there's a finance department, it's pretty easy to track down someone in that department if there is a leak in all of the shipping manifests and payment information. Yes, there is a central point of failure risk, but you have a small attack surface. You know who the few risks are.

But if you start sharing information across a broad, distributed network, there's a lot more risk. There would likely be more individuals with access to the blockchain who could share that sensitive information.

Along with your sensitive corporate or commercial data on the blockchain.

Essentially, there are critical tradeoffs in risk to consider when establishing a blockchain, in terms of how much data is available, how quickly things can be processed, and how many people will see it — or rather, how big your exposures and attack surface are.

There is one other major risk with a corporate blockchain. There is no guarantee that all of the people contributing to the blockchain will be honest with their contributions. Blockchains cannot assess the validity of the inputs. Anything that happens off the chain is subject to trust.

Someone loading agricultural goods into a shipping container still needs to be trusted by the network to provide actual and true information about the cargo that will be in transit. Without that, the information recorded in the permanent ledger is worthless.

Another example would be the chain of custody of industrial metals. Conflict metals could be mixed in with legitimate loads of metal from legal sources. This means that even if the chain of custody for the blockchain is clean, the loads could be illegal.

There is one final risk to consider about blockchains. The network that approves transactions can sometimes be driven in the wrong direction. This is effectively the risk of a tyranny of a Tocquevillian blockchain majority, whereby a network could be turned to validate improper transactions if 51 percent of the members validate them. This is called a 51 percent attack risk.

Hacking and Cryptocurrencies in Context

No one is worried about the US dollar or the Japanese yen losing value because of a hacking scandal. But this is a risk for Bitcoin and other cryptocurrencies. Exchange and wallet hacking scandals are bad for these currencies. Some libertarians argue that crypto and Bitcoin build trust in a trustless society. But that does not mean your money is safe.

There is no FDIC and SIPC to protect your crypto accounts. In the US, if a bank gets robbed, your money is still safe. The Federal Deposit Insurance Corporation (FDIC) protects deposits up to "$250,000 per depositor, per insured bank, for each account ownership category."[6] The Securities Investor Protection Service serves a similar role, protecting "$500,000, which includes a $250,000 limit for cash."[7] In 1991, The Bank of New England went bankrupt. I had a bank account at that bank. Fortunately, because of FDIC, I did not lose my money. Basically, if your bank goes bankrupt, gets robbed, or is hacked, you are covered!

But if your crypto accounts get hacked, you aren't covered.

There is no credit card dispute resolution.

Your digital key is like a bearer bond. And if someone gets it, they have your money.

Even though libertarians laud the governmentless aspect of crypto, it also means there are no safety nets. And without a safety net, the financial security of individuals is at risk. From scams. From hacks. From operator error.

CHAPTER 17

BLOCKCHAIN IN CONTEXT

The potential impact of blockchain is bigger than most people can imagine but not nearly as great as some believe. The impact on corporate supply chains in logistics, transport, and freight is going to be massive. The potential for blockchain in many corporate fields is going to be critical as well. Healthcare, agriculture, and real estate will be impacted in a big way.

But for the average person, blockchain technology is likely to be a *deus ex machina*. A god from the machine.

So, crypto is what most individuals see of blockchain now. And crypto is a special kind of *deus ex machina* — a god from the machine that also bears Lambos.

The outsized hype about blockchain has been created by the financial returns provided by cryptocurrencies. After all, there has never been a market in the history of the world with such a big financial bubble as there was at the end of 2017 and early 2018.

But crypto faces some serious challenges. And people's awareness of corporate and commercial blockchains will increase, even as cryptomania likely fades.

In order to further a discussion of the value and place in history of blockchain — from a context standpoint — I have included this chapter in the book, which also happens to include two timelines.

Make no mistake, cryptomaniacs are not to be underestimated. I was at a blockchain conference at the McCombs Business School of the University of Texas at Austin — one of the top-rated business schools in the United States — and a Bitcoin trader and investor on stage praised Bitcoin as the only true distributed blockchain. To my surprise, the gentleman sitting next to me jumped to his feet and repeatedly yelled at the top of his lungs "Preach!!!!!!" as he frenetically clapped his hands.

It was crazier than that time I got on stage to freestyle with Vanilla Ice in Raleigh, North Carolina and we couldn't get the microphone away from some crazy on stage who just wanted to say how much he loved Vanilla. Vanilla had to stop the concert.

Fortunately, the UT conference did not need to stop, but the guy next to me was, shall we say, continually vocal throughout the conference.

The high level of hype and mania around blockchain has led many people to historically contextualize blockchain in a timeline like the one in Figure 17-1 — putting blockchain along with the most critical cornerstones of historical financial record keeping.

Figure 17-1: Historical Record Keeping

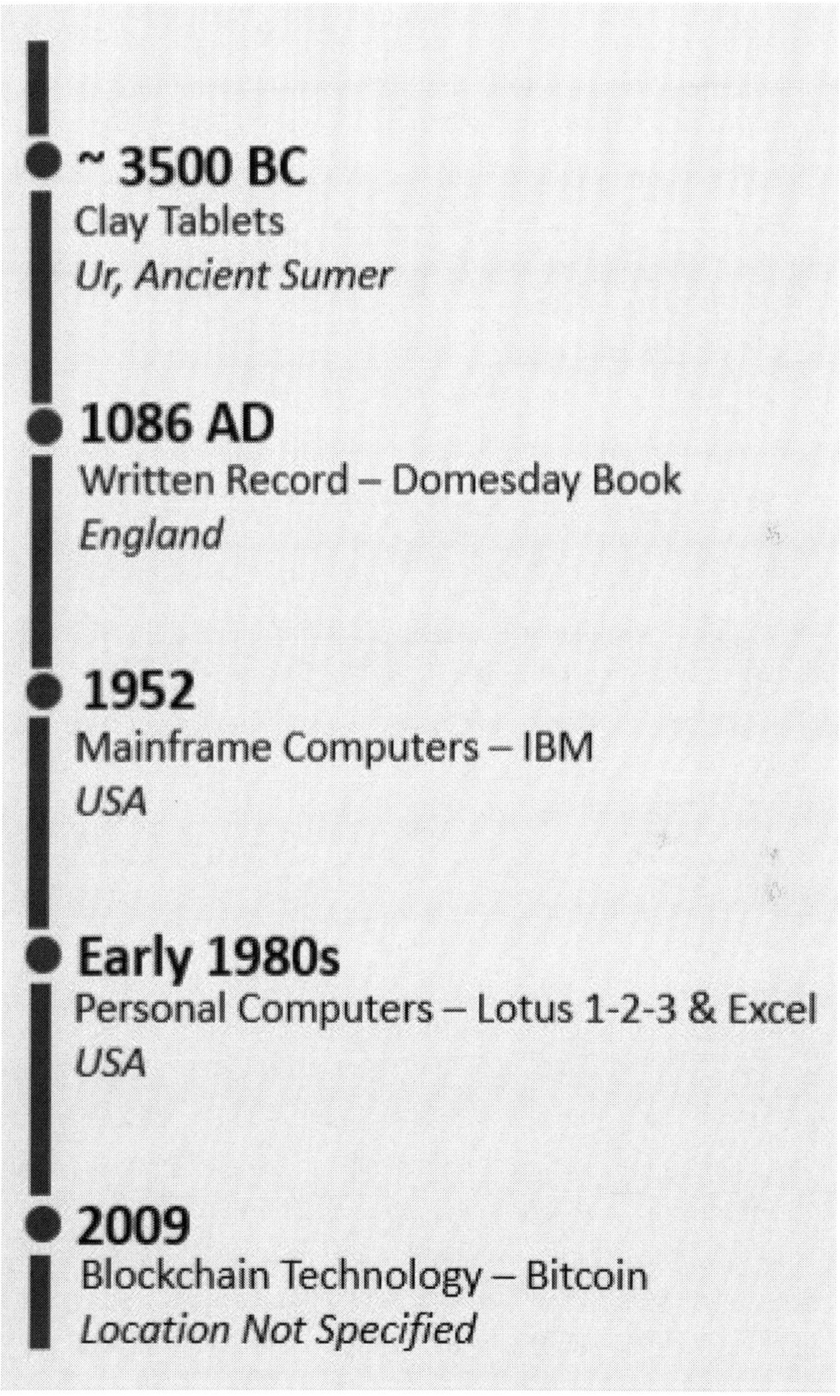

~ 3500 BC
Clay Tablets
Ur, Ancient Sumer

1086 AD
Written Record – Domesday Book
England

1952
Mainframe Computers – IBM
USA

Early 1980s
Personal Computers – Lotus 1-2-3 & Excel
USA

2009
Blockchain Technology – Bitcoin
Location Not Specified

Some of the first records of the past — well into ancient times — have been tied to recording financial transactions and assets, whether we are talking about Ancient Sumerian clay tablets at the British Museum, the Domesday Book, or the use of Lotus 1-2-3. And the same is true of Bitcoin and blockchain. These are critical accounting and financial record keeping technology disruptors. There is no doubt.

However, there is a lot more to the history of financial transactions and computerization that led to blockchain and Bitcoin than the few small historical pieces in Figure 17-1. In fact, the technological developments of computer mainframes, personal computers, software, and other technology throughout the twentieth and early twenty-first century contributed to the environment in which blockchain could be created — and could thrive. This is why I created Figure 17-2, to show how blockchain fits into these broader, recent computer, database, and technology developments.

Blockchain is a database with specialized and customized permissions, as I described in Chapter 13. And the ability to increase data transparency across a distributed network is extremely valuable. But it is not its own thing per se.

As I mentioned at other points in this book — especially Chapter 3 — blockchain technology seems like a natural extension of cloud computing. And yet it incorporates something like push technology that allows for the distributed network to receive and access a distributed ledger maintained by its decentralized nodes. In some ways, this reminds me of the Blackberry technology.

Figure 17-2: Recent Historical Technology Developments

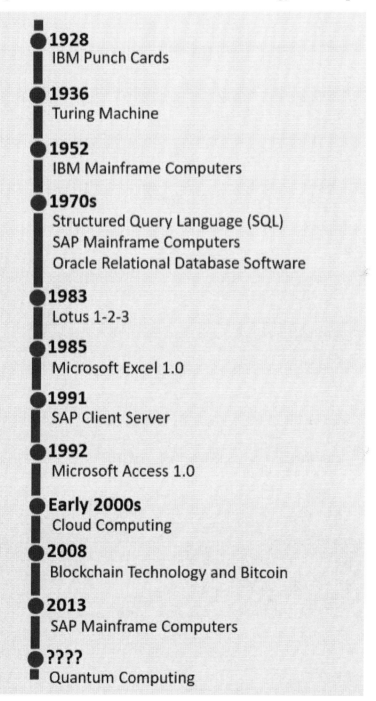

1928
IBM Punch Cards

1936
Turing Machine

1952
IBM Mainframe Computers

1970s
Structured Query Language (SQL)
SAP Mainframe Computers
Oracle Relational Database Software

1983
Lotus 1-2-3

1985
Microsoft Excel 1.0

1991
SAP Client Server

1992
Microsoft Access 1.0

Early 2000s
Cloud Computing

2008
Blockchain Technology and Bitcoin

2013
SAP Mainframe Computers

????
Quantum Computing

Interestingly, Blackberry reached its peak level of saturation in the global smartphone market in the first quarter of 2009, when 20.1 percent of smartphone operating systems were Blackberry. The first Bitcoin in the Genesis Block occurred on 3 January 2009 — during that same quarter.

It has taken time for cryptocurrencies and blockchain to catch on, but it is important to keep in mind that this is still Blackberry-era technology. Blockchain is not the end. It is a stop along the way for computing, but there is more to come. A lot more.

This leads us to the most important technology that is just around the corner: quantum computing.

Figure 17-3: Blackberry Market Saturation[1]

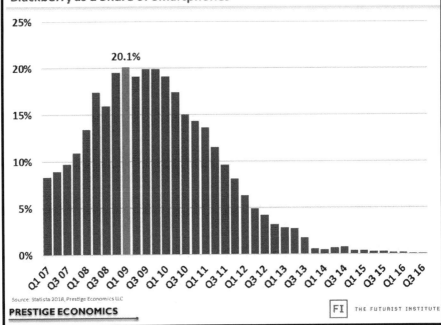

CHAPTER 18

QUANTUM COMPUTING

Quantum computing is a technology that will allow for a computational step change. Essentially all computers we use today operate on a binary computational model — 1s and 0s, like in the digital chain images on the cover of this book. This is called a bit.

But quantum computing is not just 1s and 0s, which are often seen as allegories for "on" and "off." In a quantum-computing world, there are other states of being between 1 and 0, called a *qubit*, whereby the computer is essentially in various states of both on and off at the same time.

It's kind of a tricky thing, and it's actually entwined with the multiverse theory — that there is more than one universe on any given timeline.[1] And this is tied to The University of Texas at Austin,[2] which is the same university in the city where I live — and where the blockchain conference I attended in early 2018 yielded frenzied, almost religious shrieks of "Preach!!!!!!" when Bitcoin was lauded.

As for the impact of quantum computing, adding additional states of being to the computational process may not sound like much, but the exponential impact for computing power is likely be absolutely massive — as could the implications for Bitcoin and blockchain.[3]

The cybersecurity risks I described in Chapter 16 are likely to pale in comparison to the risks to blockchains, wallets, exchanges, and cryptographic elements of cryptocurrencies in a world with quantum computing.

This is an especially noteworthy risk, because one of the things that quantum computers are likely to be exceptionally good at is cracking cryptographic problems. And this is the backbone of blockchain cryptocurrency technology.

There is a debate among theorists as to how big the impact of quantum computing could be. Some argue that blockchains and cryptocurrencies will be safe.[4] Still others propose creating quantum blockchains when this becomes an issue.[5] Since the technology does not yet exist, it is difficult to take a firm stand on this, but cybersecurity risks are unlikely to go down if computer decryption and processing power increase exponentially.

While the use cases for blockchain should now be apparent, the next technology to watch for will be quantum computing. I will be writing a future book to explore these concepts further.

THE PROMISE OF BLOCKCHAIN

I wrote this book to help put the discussion of blockchain in a context for discourse. The frenzied hype of cryptomania, may yet give way to a genuine promise of real value in the form of commercial and corporate blockchains.

The image on the cover of the burning of the ancient Library of Alexandria highlights one of the greatest value propositions for blockchains — a reduction in the risk associated with a central point of failure. In describing the loss at the Library of Alexandria, Pollard and Reed noted that, "What had taken a lifetime to learn, Caesar could destroy in a morning with little more than a torch."[1]

Companies are exposed to central points of failure, and blockchain technology could reduce those risks by sharing information across a distributed network. But this is not without risks, as it would increase the attack surface of the entity using the blockchain, which is a critical issue for cybersecurity.

While blockchains are likely to move forward, cryptocurrencies, and Bitcoin in particular, face significant risks.

As a futurist, I believe it is important to place technological developments in a historical context. And blockchain is just one of the newest of many recordkeeping database technologies. And it is highly unlikely to be the last,

For now, blockchain technology offers the hope and promise of distributed information and knowledge that can reduce costs, add economic value, and prevent a Library of Alexandria-level loss of information and institutional knowledge for corporate, governmental, and private entities.

And yet blockchain is also the hype. It has been tied to the biggest investment bubble in the history of the world. And when it is used for unregulated cryptocurrency transactions, it could be the fire that threatens to destroy civilization by allowing for terrorists, anarchists, mobsters, and politically subversive entities to thrive.

That is why I see so much promise for blockchain as an emerging disruptive technology.

And why I see both the hope and the hype.

BLOCKCHAIN GLOSSARY

Altcoin — Digital currencies that have been independently constructed on their own blockchains or that have been created using an existing blockchain network like Ethereum.

Bloat — Increasing size of the Bitcoin blockchain. As of August 2018, it was 125 GB. It is expected to increase in size significantly in the future.

Blockchain — A distributed ledger technology that functions as the underlying framework for Bitcoin and other digital currencies.

Bitcoin (BTC) — One of the first digital currencies, built on a blockchain using a distributed network of nodes. It is abbreviated as BTC for trading purposes.

Central Point of Failure (CPOF) — A special kind of single point of failure, whereby a network is at risk of failure due to its centralization of entire operations, record keeping, or authority.

Cryptocurrency — A currency that is not backed by a central bank. It has been created independently.

dApp — Decentralized application. A *dApp* has its backend code running on a decentralized peer-to-peer network.

Distributed Ledger Technology (DLT) — The record of transactions on a blockchain that is distributed to its network of nodes. DLT should not suffer from central point of failure risk.

HODL — Phrase used by cryptocurrency and Bitcoin fans to denote holding onto cryptocurrency even as price drops and to not sell — no matter what. This is often used with a meme from the movie *300* about the unrelenting defense of Sparta.

ICO — Initial Coin Offering. This is a way in which companies issue new cryptocurrency coins that can be used for trading. It is also a way they can issue coins and utility tokens that will offer some utility and the ability to use their platform or startup endeavor at some point in the future. ICOs are often done after a white paper, and they are usually implemented by companies that are pre-revenue and not yet operational. This pre-revenue funding activity is how ICOs are like crowdfunding.

Ethereum (ETH) — A main altcoin, abbreviated for trading purposes as ETH. Ethereum is the VHS of cryptocurrencies, in that other coins can easily use its interface and platform for the purpose of creating other altcoins and utility tokens. These coins can have whatever name the creator chooses. Some even have obscene names.

Litecoin (LTC) — An early altcoin, abbreviated as LTC for trading purposes.

Mining — The process of solving a hash puzzle and adding a block to the blockchain by using computational processing power that results in an award.

Nodes — Distributed parts of a blockchain network. They can process the transactions within the network.

Ripple (XRP) — An altcoin designed to make cross-border payments more efficient. It is abbreviated as XRP for trading purposes.

Satoshi — Satoshi Nakamoto. This is the name of the founder of Bitcoin and the first proponent of blockchain technology on which Bitcoin operates.

Single Point of Failure (SPOF) — The risk that an entire network or entity could fail due to weakness at one point somewhere in the network. Examples would be power transformers and internet routers.

When Moon? When Lambo? — Phrase used by cryptocurrency fans to ask when a cryptocurrency will rise so much that it will go to the moon and they can buy a Lamborghini.

White Paper — The main way to promote an altcoin or ICO. This was pioneered by Satoshi.

ENDNOTES

Chapter 3

1. Dan, A. and Rico, C. eds. (2017). *The Library of Alexandria: A Cultural Crossroads of the Ancient World: Proceedings of the Second Polis Institute Interdisciplinary Conference*. Jerusalem, Israel: The Polis Institute. Also see Charles River Editors. *The Library of Alexandria*. Young University Press. Also see El-Abbadi, M. (Apr 13, 2018) "Library of Alexandria" Encyclopedia Britannica. Retrieved on August 24, 2018 from https://www.britannica.com/topic/Library-of-Alexandria.

2. Plutarch (2017). The Age of Caesar: Five Roman Lives. Translated by Pamela Mensch. P. 146.

3. Göll, H. (1876). *Galerie der Meister in Wissenscheft und Kunst. Meister der Wissenschaft I. Die Weisen und Gelehrten des Altherthums*. Second Edition. Leipzig: Verlag von Otto Spamer. P. 395

Chapter 4

1. Satoshi, N. (2008). *Bitcoin: A Peer-to-Peer Electronic Cash System.* P. 1. Retrieved from https://bitcoin.org/bitcoin.pdf.

2. "Internal-Combustion Engine." *The Columbia Encyclopedia, 6th ed.* Retrieved on 24 August 2018 from https://www.encyclopedia.com/science-and-technology/technology/technology-terms-and-concepts/internal-combustion-engine.

3. Licensed from Adobe Stock.

Chapter 5

1. "Genesis Block" Wikipedia. Bitcoin Wiki. Retrieved on 24 August 2018 from https://en.bitcoin.it/wiki/Main_Page.

2. Bank of England, Total Central Bank Assets for United Kingdom (DISCONTINUED) [UKASSETS], retrieved from FRED, Federal Reserve Bank of St. Louis; https://fred.stlouisfed.org/series/UKASSETS, 24 August 2018.

3. European Central Bank, Central Bank Assets for Euro Area (11-19 Countries) [ECBASSETS], retrieved from FRED, Federal Reserve Bank of St. Louis; https://fred.stlouisfed.org/series/ECBASSETS, 24 August 2018.

4. "Balance Sheets of the Bank of Japan and Financial Insititutions." Bank of Japan, Retrieved on 24 August 2018 from https://www.boj.or.jp/en/statistics/category/financial.htm/.

5. Pretov, A. (2017). "ETFs in Monetary Policy – Case Study: Bank of Japan." State Street Global Advisors. Retrieved on 24 August 2018 from https://www.swfinstitute.org/content/ID11548-INST-8354_ETFs-in-Monetary-Policy_web_FINAL.pdf. Fueda-Samikawa, I. (2017) "BOJ's ETF Purchases Expanding Steadily" Japan Center for Economic Research. Retrieved on 24 August 2018 from https://www.jcer.or.jp/eng/pdf/170706_report(eng).pdf.

(2018). "BOJ Kuroda: Japan Economic Conditions Fine Despite Stock Fall" Market News. Retrieved on 24 August 2018 from https://www.marketnews.com/content/boj-kuroda-japan-economic-conditions-fine-despite-stock-fall.

6. Board of Governors of the Federal Reserve System (US), All Federal Reserve Banks: Total Assets [WALCL], retrieved from FRED, Federal Reserve Bank of St. Louis; https://fred.stlouisfed.org/series/WALCL, 24 August 2018.

7. Yellen, J. (26 August 2016). "*The Federal Reserve's Monetary Policy Toolkit: Past, Present, and Future.*" US Federal Reserve. Retrieved from https://www.federalreserve.gov/newsevents/speech/yellen20160826a.htm

8. Retrieved on 26 August 2018 from http://www.usdebtclock.org/.

9. U.S. Department of the Treasury. Fiscal Service, Federal Debt: Total Public Debt [GFDEBTN], retrieved from FRED, Federal Reserve Bank of St. Louis; https://fred.stlouisfed.org/series/GFDEBTN, 24 August 2018.

10. Federal Reserve Bank of St. Louis and U.S. Office of Management and Budget, Federal Debt: Total Public Debt as Percent of Gross Domestic Product [GFDEGDQ188S], retrieved from FRED, Federal Reserve Bank of St. Louis; https://fred.stlouisfed.org/series/GFDEGDQ188S, 24 August 2018.

11. Desjardins, J. (6 August 2015). "$60 Trillion of World Debt in One Visualization." Visual Capitalist. Retrieved 11 February 2017: http://www.visualcapitalist.com/60-trillion-of-world-debt-in-one-visualization/.

12. Mayer, J. (18 November 18 2015). "The Social Security Façade." Retrieved 11 February 2017: http://www.usnews.com/opinion/economic-intelligence/2015/11/18/social-security-and-medicare-have-morphed-into-unsustainable-entitlements.

13. Image provided courtesy of The Heritage Foundation. Retrieved 11 February 2017: http://thf_media.s3.amazonaws.com/infographics/2014/10/BG-eliminate-waste-control-spending-chart-3_HIGHRES.jpg.

14. US Social Security Administration. "Social Security History: Otto von Bismarck." Sourced from https://www.ssa.gov/history/ottob.html.

15. Twarog, S. (January 1997). "Heights and Living Standards in Germany, 1850-1939: The Case of Wurttemberg" as reprinted in *Health and Welfare During Industrialization.* Steckel, R. and F. Roderick eds. Chicago: University of Chicago Press, p. 315. Retrieved 11 February 2017: http://www.nber.org/chapters/c7434.pdf.

16. US Social Security Administration. *Fast Facts and Figures About Social Security, 2017,* p.8. Retrieved on 6 June 2018: https://www.ssa.gov/policy/docs/chartbooks/fast_facts/.

17. World Bank, Population Growth for the United States [SPPOPGROWUSA], retrieved from FRED, Federal Reserve Bank of St. Louis; https://fred.stlouisfed.org/series/SPPOPGROWUSA, 24 August 2018.

18. Last, J. (2013) *What to Expect, When No One's Expecting: America's Coming Demographic Disaster.* New York: Encounter Books., pp. 2-4.

19. Ibid., p. 3.

Chapter 6
1. Hayek, F.A. (1976). *The Denationalization of Money.* London: The Institute of Economic Affairs, pp. 130-131.

2. Ibid., p. 130.

3. Gold price data from the London Bullion Market Association as sourced from MacroTrends Data. Additional data sourced from eSignal.

4. Hayek, F.A. (1979). "A Free-Market Monetary System and the Pretense of Knowledge," p. 23.

Chapter 7
1. Covering the Crisis: The role of media in the financial crisis. European Journalism Centre. 2010.

2. Ibid., p. 75.

3. Ibid., p. 81.

4. "Bitcoin (USD) Price." Coindesk. Retrieved on 24 August 2018 from https://www.coindesk.com/price/.

5. Owen, D. (2005). "The Betamax vs BHS Format War." Media College. Retrieved on 24 August 2018 from https://www.mediacollege.com/video/format/compare/betamax-vhs.html.

6. ICO meme as seen on the internet.

7. Schor, L. (2018) "ICO Market Report (April 2018)" Argon Group. Retrieved on 24 August 2018 from https://medium.com/@argongroup/ico-market-report-april-2018-3857cbe729c3.

8. Ibid.

9. Ibid.

10. Ibid.

11 ICO meme as seen on the internet.

Chapter 8

1. Goodman, G. (1981). "Commanding Heights" Public Broadcasting Service. Retrieved on 24 August 2018 from http://www.pbs.org/wgbh/commandingheights/shared/minitext/ess_germanhyperinflation.html.

2. Cancel, D (2018). "Venezuela Currency Chaos So Bad, There's an App to Lop Off Zeros." Bloomberg News. Retrieved on 24 August 2018 from https://www.bloomberg.com/news/articles/2018-08-23/confused-by-venezuela-s-currency-chaos-there-s-an-app-for-that.

Chapter 9

1. Farley, A. (2018). "Bearer Bonds: From Popular to Prohibited" Investopedia. Retrieved on 24 August 2018 from https://www.investopedia.com/articles/bonds/08/bearer-bond.asp.

2. Image provided courtesy of Heritage Auctions, HA.com. Retrieved on 24 August 2018 from https://currency.ha.com/itm/miscellaneous/other/-1-000-000-us-treasury-bearer-bond/a/364-15547.s.

Chapter 10

1. (2018) "Frequently Asked Questions" bitcoin.org. Retrieved on 24 August 2018 from https://bitcoin.org/en/faq#general.

2. Cheng, E. (2018). "There are now 17 million bitcoins in existence – only 4 million left to 'mine'." CNBC. Retrieved on 24 August 2018 from https://www.cnbc.com/2018/04/26/there-are-now-17-million-bitcoins-in-existence--only-4-million-left-to-mine.html.

3. This is some additional Faustian wordplay. See under Goethe, J.W. (1808). *Faust.*

4. "Gasoline Prices Around the World: The Real Cost of Filling Up." (July 25, 2018) Bloomberg News. Retrieved on 24 August 2018 from https://www.bloomberg.com/graphics/gas-prices/#20182:Australia:USD:g.

5. "Annual Energy Outlook 2018." (2018). U.S. Energy Information Administration. Retrieved on 24 August 2018 from https://www.eia.gov/outlooks/aeo/pdf/AEO2018.pdf.

Chapter 11

1. "Annual Economics Report." (June 2018). Bank of International Settlements, p.91-141. Retrieved from https://www.bis.org/publ/arpdf/ar2018e.pdf.

2. "Transaction Speeds: How Do Cryptocurrencies Stack Up To Visa or PayPal?" (10 January 2018). howmuch.net. Retrieved on 24 August 2018 from https://howmuch.net/sources/crypto-transaction-speeds-compared.

Chapter 12

1. Lagarde, C (26 April 2018). "Statement by IMF Managing Director Christine Lagarde on Her Participation in the Paris Conference on Terrorism Financing" International Monetary Fund. Retrieved on 24 August 2018 from https://www.imf.org/en/News/Articles/2018/04/26/pr18150-lagarde-on-her-participation-in-the-paris-conference-on-terrorism-financing.
2. "Annual Economics Report." (June 2018). Bank of International Settlements, p.91-141. Retrieved from https://www.bis.org/publ/arpdf/ar2018e.pdf.

Chapter 13

1. Carson, B. (June 2018). "Blockchain beyond the hype: What is the strategic business value?" McKinsey & Company. Retrieved on August 28, 2018 from https://www.mckinsey.com/business-functions/digital-mckinsey/our-insights/blockchain-beyond-the-hype-what-is-the-strategic-business-value.
2. "#BLOCKCHAIN: Back-office block-buster" Autonomous Research. Retrieved on 24 August 2018 from https://next.autonomous.com/blockchain-blockbuster/.

Chapter 14

1. "The Yellow Book" (2018). U.S. Government Accountability Office. Retrieved on 24 August 2018 from https://www.gao.gov/yellowbook/overview.
2. "Estonia becomes first nation with mobile voting." (12 December 2008) TechCrunch. Retrieved on 24 August 2018 from https://techcrunch.com/2008/12/12/estonia-becomes-first-nation-with-mobile-voting/.

Chapter 15

1. "Widespread Fraud Found in Cryptocurrency Offerings." (April 10, 2018). Texas State Securities Board. Retrieved on 24 August 2018 from https://www.ssb.texas.gov/sites/default/files/CRYPTO%20report%20April%2010%202018.pdf.
2. "Bitcoin (USD) Price" coindesk. Retrieved on 24 August 2018 from https://www.coindesk.com/price/.
3. "What is Bitcoin? Google Trends Search" Google Trends. Retrieved on 24 August 2018 from https://trends.google.com/trends/explore?q=What%20is%20Bitcoin%3F&geo=US.
4. "Confirmed Transactions Per Day." (2018). Blockchain. Retrieved on 24 August 2018 from https://www.blockchain.com/charts/n-transactions.
5. Schor, L. (2018). "ICO Market Report (April 2018)" Argon Group. Retrieved on 24 August 2018 from https://medium.com/@argongroup/ico-market-report-april-2018-3857cbe729c3.
6. Ibid.
7. Schenker, J. (9 July 2017). "Does Your Dog Need a Podcast?" LinkedIn. Retrieved on 24 August 2018 from https://www.linkedin.com/pulse/does-your-dog-need-podcast-jason-schenker/.
8. Schor, L. (2018). "ICO Market Report (April 2018)" Argon Group. Retrieved on 24 August 2018 from https://medium.com/@argongroup/ico-market-report-april-2018-3857cbe729c3.
9. Ibid.
10. Katz, L. (August 1, 2018). "Long Blockchain Gets Hit With SEC Subpoena After Nasdaq Ouster." Bloomberg News. Retrieved on 24 August 2018 from https://www.bloomberg.com/news/articles/2018-08-01/long-blockchain-gets-hit-with-sec-subpoena-after-nasdaq-ouster.

Chapter 16

1. Satoshi, N. (2008). *Bitcoin: A Peer-to-Peer Electronic Cash System.* P. 1. Retrieved from https://bitcoin.org/bitcoin.pdf.

2. "Annual Economics Report." (June 2018). Bank of International Settlements, p. 107. Retrieved on 24 August 2018 from https://www.bis.org/publ/arpdf/ar2018e.pdf.

3. "Managing the Risks of Cryptocurrency." (2018). BAE Systems. Retrieved on 24 August 2018 from https://www.baesystems.com/en/cybersecurity/managing-the-risks-of-cryptocurrency.

4. "How Criminals Steal Cryptocurrency (InfoGraphic)." CryptoGo. Retrieved on 24 August 2018 from https://josephsteinberg.com/how-criminals-steal-cryptocurrency-infographic/.

5. "Understanding Deposit Insurance." (2018). Federal Deposit Insurance Corporation. Retrieved on 24 August 2018 from https://www.fdic.gov/deposit/deposits/.

6. "What SIPC Protects." Securities Investor Protection Corporation. Retrieved on 24 August 2018 from https://www.sipc.org/for-investors/what-sipc-protects.

Chapter 17

1. "Global smartphone OS market share held by RIM (BlackBerry) from 2007 to 2016, by quarter" Statista. Retrieved on 24 August 2018 from https://www.statista.com/statistics/263439/global-market-share-held-by-rim-smartphones/.

Chapter 18

1. Gribbin, J. (2014). Computing with Quantum Cats. Amherst, New York: Prometheus Books, pp. 183-225.

2. Ibid.

3. Friedson, I. (28 February 2018). "How Quantum Computing Threatens Blockchain." National Review. Retrieved on 24 August 2018 from https://www.nationalreview.com/2018/02/quantum-computing-blockchain-technology-threat/. See also arXIV. (8 November 2017) "Quantum Computers Post Imminent Threat to Bitcoin Security" Technology Review. Retrieved on 24 August 2018 from https://www.technologyreview.com/s/609408/quantum-computers-pose-imminent-threat-to-bitcoin-security/.

4. Brennen, G (18 October 2017). "Quantum attacks on bitcoin, and how to protect against them." Cornell University Library. Retrieved on 24 August 2018 from https://arxiv.org/abs/1710.10377.

5. arXIV. (1 May 2018). "If quantum computers threaten blockchains, quantum blockchains could be the defense" Technology Review. Retrieved on 24 August 2018 from https://www.technologyreview.com/s/611022/if-quantum-computers-threaten-blockchains-quantum-blockchains-could-be-the-defense/.

Conclusion

1. Pollard, J. and Reid, H. (2007). *The Rise and Fall of Alexandria: Birthplace of the Modern World.* New York: Penguin Books, p. 165.

ABOUT THE AUTHOR

Jason Schenker is the President of Prestige Economics and the world's top-ranked financial market futurist. Bloomberg News has ranked Mr. Schenker one of the most accurate forecasters in the world in 42 different categories since 2011, including #1 in the world in 25 categories for his forecasts of the Euro, the Pound, the Swiss Franc, the Chinese RMB, crude oil prices, natural gas prices, gold prices, industrial metals prices, agricultural prices, US non-farm payrolls, and US new home sales.

Mr. Schenker has written nine books, four of which have been #1 Best Sellers on Amazon: *Commodity Prices 101*, *Recession-Proof*, *Electing Recession*, and *Jobs for Robots*. He also edited the #1 Best Seller *The Robot and Automation Almanac—2018*. Mr. Schenker is also a columnist for *Bloomberg Opinion*. Mr. Schenker has appeared as a guest and guest host on Bloomberg Television as well as a guest on CNBC. He is frequently quoted in the press, including *The Wall Street Journal, The New York Times*, and *The Financial Times*.

Prior to founding Prestige Economics, Mr. Schenker worked for McKinsey & Company as a Risk Specialist, where he directed trading and risk initiatives on six continents. Before joining McKinsey, Mr. Schenker worked for Wachovia as an Economist.

Mr. Schenker holds a Master's in Applied Economics from UNC Greensboro, a Master's in Negotiation from CSU Dominguez Hills, a Master's in German from UNC Chapel Hill, and a Bachelor's with distinction in History and German from The University of Virginia. He also holds a certificate in FinTech from MIT, an executive certificate in Supply Chain Management from MIT, a graduate certificate in Professional Development from UNC, an executive certificate in Negotiation from Harvard Law School, and a certificate in Cybersecurity with NACD and Carnegie Mellon University. Mr. Schenker holds the professional designations CMT® (Chartered Market Technician), CVA® (Certified Valuation Analyst), ERP® (Energy Risk Professional), CFP® (Certified Financial Planner), and FLTA (Certified Futurist and Long-Term Analyst). Mr. Schenker is also an instructor for LinkedIn Learning. His course on Financial Risk Management was released in October 2017, and his weekly Economic Indicator Series was released in 2018.

Mr. Schenker is a member of the Texas Business Leadership Council, the only CEO-based public policy research organization in Texas, with a limited membership of 100 CEOs and Presidents. He is also a member of the 2018 Director class of the Texas Lyceum, a non-partisan, non-profit that fosters business and policy dialogue on important US and Texas issues.

Mr. Schenker is an active executive in FinTech as a member of the Central Texas Angel Network and as the Executive Director of the Texas Blockchain Association. He is also a member of the National Association of Corporate Directors as well as an NACD Board Governance Fellow.

In October 2016, Mr. Schenker founded The Futurist Institute to help analysts, strategists, and economists become futurists through a training and certification program.

Mr. Schenker was ranked one of the top 100 most influential financial advisors in the world by Investopedia in June 2018.

For more information about Jason Schenker:

www.jasonschenker.com

For more information about The Futurist Institute:

www.futuristinstitute.org

For more information about Prestige Economics:

www.prestigeeconomics.com

TOP FORECASTER ACCURACY RANKINGS

Prestige Economics has been recognized as the most accurate independent commodity and financial market research firm in the world. As the only forecaster for Prestige Economics, Jason Schenker is very proud that Bloomberg News has ranked him a top forecaster in 42 different categories since 2011, including #1 in the world in 25 different forecast categories.

Mr. Schenker has been top ranked as a forecaster of economic indicators, energy prices, metals prices, agricultural prices, and foreign exchange rates.

ECONOMIC TOP RANKINGS

#1 Non-Farm Payroll Forecaster in the World
#1 New Home Sales Forecaster in the World
#2 US Unemployment Rate Forecaster in the World
#3 Durable Goods Orders Forecaster in the World
#6 Consumer Confidence Forecaster in the World
#7 ISM Manufacturing Index Forecaster in the World
#7 US Housing Start Forecaster in the World

ENERGY PRICE TOP RANKINGS

#1 WTI Crude Oil Price Forecaster in the World

#1 Brent Crude Oil Price Forecaster in the World

#1 Henry Hub Natural Gas Price Forecaster in the World

METALS PRICE TOP RANKINGS

#1 Gold Price Forecaster in the World

#1 Platinum Price Forecaster in the World

#1 Palladium Price Forecaster in the World

#1 Industrial Metals Price Forecaster in the World

#1 Copper Price Forecaster in the World

#1 Aluminum Price Forecaster in the World

#1 Nickel Price Forecaster in the World

#1 Tin Price Forecaster in the World

#1 Zinc Price Forecaster in the World

#2 Precious Metals Price Forecaster in the World

#2 Silver Price Forecaster in the World

#2 Lead Price Forecaster in the World

#2 Iron Ore Forecaster in the World

AGRICULTURAL PRICE TOP RANKINGS

#1 Coffee Price Forecaster in the World

#1 Cotton Price Forecaster in the World

#1 Sugar Price Forecaster in the World

#1 Soybean Price Forecaster in the World

FOREIGN EXCHANGE TOP RANKINGS

#1 Euro Forecaster in the World

#1 British Pound Forecaster in the World

#1 Swiss Franc Forecaster in the World

#1 Chinese RMB Forecaster in the World

#1 Russian Ruble Forecaster in the World

#1 Brazilian Real Forecaster in the World

#3 Major Currency Forecaster in the World

#3 Canadian Dollar Forecaster in the World

#4 Japanese Yen Forecaster in the World

#5 Australian Dollar Forecaster in the World

#7 Mexican Peso Forecaster in the World

#1 EURCHF Forecaster in the World

#2 EURJPY Forecaster in the World

#2 EURGBP Forecaster in the World

#2 EURRUB Forecaster in the World

ABOUT THE PUBLISHER

Prestige Professional Publishing LLC was founded in 2011 to produce insightful and timely professional reference books. We are registered with the Library of Congress.

Published Titles

Be The Shredder, Not The Shred

Commodity Prices 101

Electing Recession

Jobs for Robots

Robot-Proof Yourself

The Robot and Automation Almanac — 2018

Midterm Economics

The Promise of Blockchain

Future Titles

Spikes: Growth Hacking Leadership

The Brain Business

The Valuation Onion

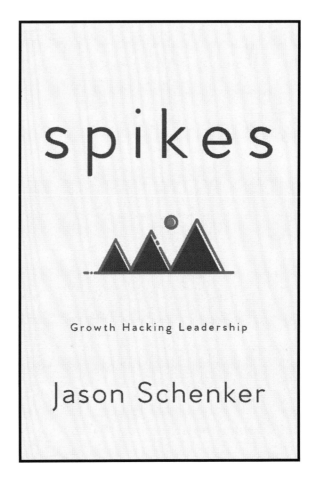

Spikes: Growth Hacking Leadership presents proactive strategies to help individuals advance rapidly in their professional careers by hacking the system. This book is slated to be published in early 2019 by Prestige Professional Publishing.

— THE ROBOT AND AUTOMATION ALMANAC —

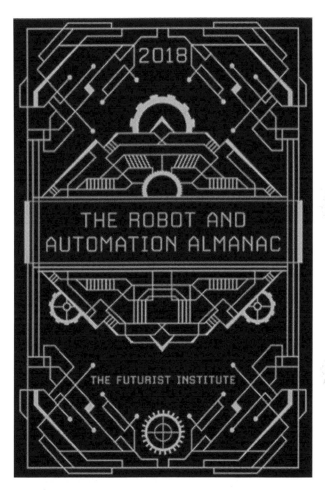

The Robot and Automation Almanac: 2018 is a collection of essays by robot and automation experts, executives, and investors on the big trends to watch for in automation and robotics. *The Robot and Automation Almanac: 2018* was compiled by The Futurist Institute and published by Prestige Professional Publishing in January 2018. This book has been a #1 Best Seller on Amazon.

Robot-Proof Yourself offers a number of practical professional recommendations for how to be robot-proof in the coming era of professional, economic, and financial disruptions. Robots and automation are set to advance, but individuals have a chance to benefit from the coming changes. *Robot-Proof Yourself* was released in December 2017.

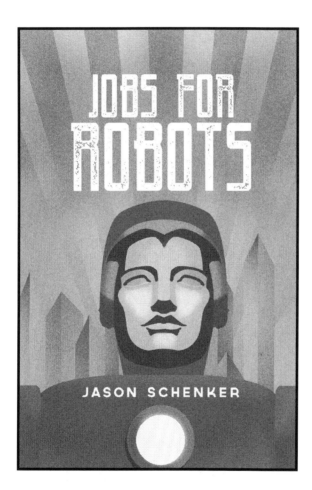

Jobs for Robots provides an in-depth look at the future of automation and robots, with a focus on the opportunities as well as the risks ahead. Job creation in coming years will be extremely strong for the kind of workers that do not require payroll taxes, health care, or vacation: robots. *Jobs for Robots* was published in February 2017. This book has been a #1 Best Seller on Amazon.

DISCLAIMER

FROM THE AUTHOR

The following disclaimer applies to any content in this book:

This book is commentary intended for general information use only and is not investment advice. Jason Schenker does not make recommendations on any specific or general investments, investment types, asset classes, non-regulated markets, specific equities, bonds, or other investment vehicles. Jason Schenker does not guarantee the completeness or accuracy of analyses and statements in this book, nor does Jason Schenker assume any liability for any losses that may result from the reliance by any person or entity on this information. Opinions, forecasts, and information are subject to change without notice. This book does not represent a solicitation or offer of financial or advisory services or products; this book is only market commentary intended and written for general information use only. This book does not constitute investment advice.

DISCLAIMER

FROM THE PUBLISHER

The following disclaimer applies to any content in this book:

This book is commentary intended for general information use only and is not investment advice. Prestige Professional Publishing LLC does not make recommendations on any specific or general investments, investment types, asset classes, non-regulated markets, specific equities, bonds, or other investment vehicles. Prestige Professional Publishing LLC does not guarantee the completeness or accuracy of analyses and statements in this book, nor does Prestige Professional Publishing LLC assume any liability for any losses that may result from the reliance by any person or entity on this information. Opinions, forecasts, and information are subject to change without notice. This book does not represent a solicitation or offer of financial or advisory services or products; this book is only market commentary intended and written for general information use only. This book does not constitute investment advice.

Prestige Professional Publishing LLC

7101 Fig Vine Cove

Austin, Texas 78750

www.prestigeprofessionalpublishing.com

ISBN: 978-1-946197-10-8 *Paperback*
           978-1-946197-11-5 *Ebook*

Made in the USA
Columbia, SC
27 February 2019